DISCOVER
DOUGH CRAFT

DISCOVER
DOUGH CRAFT

40 ORIGINAL PROJECTS TO BUILD YOUR MODELLING SKILLS

SOPHIE-JANE PRIOR
AND
SUSAN WELBY

HAMLYN

First published in Great Britain in 1994 by Hamlyn
an imprint of Reed Consumer Books Limited,
Michelin House, 81 Fulham Road, London SW3 6RB
and Auckland, Melbourne, Singapore and Toronto
Reprinted 1995
TEXT AND PHOTOGRAPHS © 1994
REED INTERNATIONAL BOOKS LIMITED

SERIES EDITOR: **JONATHAN HILTON**
SERIES ART EDITOR: **PRUE BUCKNELL**
ART EDITOR: **ALISON SHACKLETON**
EXECUTIVE EDITOR: **JUDITH MORE**
ART DIRECTOR: **JACQUI SMALL**

PHOTOGRAPHS BY: **LUCY MASON**

The publishers have made every effort to ensure that all instructions
given in this book are accurate and safe, but they cannot accept liability
for any resulting injury, damage or loss to either person or property
whether direct or consequential and howsoever arising. The author and
publishers will be grateful for any information which will assist them in
keeping future editions up to date.

ISBN: 0 60058 303 1

DTP ALISON SHACKLETON
ORIGINATION BY MANDARIN, SINGAPORE
PRINTED AND BOUND IN HONG KONG

CONTENTS

INTRODUCTION

It's impossible to be precise about the origins of salt dough. Bread has been a staple food in millions of homes for thousands of years – combine this with the creative impulse that makes decoration such a deep-set tradition worldwide and it is easy to see why fashioning objects from dough is a craft practised by so many nations.

We know that the ancient Egyptians, Romans and Greeks made dough-figure offerings to their gods and making dough decorations to commemorate religious festivals – particularly Christmas – is still popular in many European countries. Brightly coloured dough models are available on market stalls in South America, and tourist centres in Shanghai still demonstrate the traditional art of making dolls from twists of dyed dough. Salt-dough modelling is enjoying a revival in the United States, and dough objects are beginning to make an appearance in British gift shops and craft fairs once again. So, although it is more popular in some places than others, no single country seems to be able to claim the craft as an invention. According to some experts, adding salt to the dough mixture began when decorating Christmas trees became fashionable in Germany in the 1800s as a way of discouraging mice and rats from eating the dough.

Traditional arts and crafts rise and fall in popularity and the availability of more sophisticated modelling materials, like ready-made and non-bake clays may have contributed to the decline in popularity of salt dough. Convenience is bound to be appealing but price can be restricting, especially where size and quantity are concerned. Salt dough is just as adaptable as these materials and a lot cheaper to use in bulk.

THE INSPIRATION

One morning, a few weeks before Christmas, a neighbour gave Sophie-Jane Prior a home-baked and glazed salt-dough wreath. Inspired by the simplicity of the idea – and the fact that she had not yet decorated the house for

Christmas – Sophie asked for the recipe and began making her own wreaths and decorations. Months later, and more enthusiastic than ever, she had moved on. After making an assortment of simple, egg-glazed wreaths, Sophie experimented with colours, shapes and surface textures. Soon she had made enough plaques, relief-work pots and ornately framed mirrors to stock a stall at the local craft fair. The salt-dough objects sold in a few hours. Customers weren't just enthusiastic, they were also curious. "Were they really made from bread?" "Could you bake them in an ordinary oven?" "What kind of paint did you use?"

This book aims to answer these questions and many more. The practical side of salt-dough modelling is covered by the materials and techniques section, which should give you a clear idea of the technicalities involved. Refer to this section whenever you have doubts about recipes, timings, repairing cracks, building relief patterns, and so on. The crafts are not just decorative – they are designed to inspire you to make your way through each section, acquiring skill and confidence as you go. The models themselves, however, are to provide ideas, not hard-and-fast rules.

You will find suggestions about paint effects, textures, cut-outs and alternative ways of achieving finishes in the introductions to most projects. Use the illustrations and instructions as guidelines, but let your imagination be the final arbiter. None of the projects involves intricate or fiddly paint techniques or modelling and apart from standard items used for each project – which can be found in most kitchens – the equipment required is easily obtainable.

Don't feel that you have to follow every instruction to the letter; you will get as much enjoyment from adding your own variations as you would from reproducing the crafts exactly as illustrated. And you don't need any particular artistic ability to make these designs. Aiming for perfection can be inhibiting, so relax and try not to see every flaw as a failure. Production-line perfection is not inspiring and it often lacks the charm of a hand-made craft!

MATERIALS AND TECHNIQUES

It goes without saying that you want your dough craft to look as good as possible – but don't be discouraged if any unexpected results should occur. Small flaws can add interesting dimensions to a project, and an "accident" may produce an original texture or unusual surface finish. If you highlight rather than hide these quirks, the object becomes original and unique to you. Nobody is suggesting that you should settle for second best – but think twice before throwing away your mistakes.

MAKING THE DOUGH

The dough used for all the project work in this book is salt dough. Some salt dough experts include a tablespoon of cooking oil for a "smoother, stronger blend", while others would not dream of mixing dough without adding a couple of heaped tablespoons of wallpaper paste, which make the dough more elastic to model and quicker to air-dry (*see p. 13*).

This book, however, uses traditional salt dough – not only is it easier to stay with just a single recipe, but when it is made up and handled properly, a simple salt-flour-water mix is very successful, extremely adaptable and behaves with a certain predictability, which is reassuring when you are embarking on new projects!

The recipe given here makes up enough dough for one smallish project and two of the larger ones – a few small, individual decorations, for example, as well as two soup bowl-sized models with relief work. This may seem a lot, but using the oven to bake more than one object at a time makes good economical, and ecological, sense.

If you require less or more dough, then simply halve or double the amounts given accordingly. Bear in mind that, as a general rule, you should always use half the amount of salt to flour.

THE INGREDIENTS
● Flour – Plain white flour has been used throughout this book. Use good-quality flour – cheaper brands may be difficult to handle and they may also vary widely in their degree of absorbency. Wholemeal types of flour may produce interesting textured effects, but they are heavier to handle and take longer to bake or to air-dry. But this this does not rule them out. Self-raising flour puffs up in the oven and therefore should never be used for dough craft modelling.
● Salt – As long as the salt has been finely ground, the cheapest brand available is perfectly adequate to make good dough.

YOU WILL NEED
● Large mixing bowl
● Coffee mug
● Water jug
● Cool surface for kneading

THE BASIC RECIPE

● Two level mugs of plain white flour
● One level mug of finely ground salt
Pour the ingredients into a large mixing bowl and combine them thoroughly.

MIXING
Gradually add sufficient lukewarm water to knead the mixture into a pliable ball. This should take approximately 12fl oz (355ml) of water, but you will need to judge the exact amount by "feel". If the mixture becomes too sticky, add a little more flour; if it crumbles, add more water.

DOUGH TIPS

● To make dough paste, take some raw dough and mix it with sufficient water to resemble single cream. If necessary, vary this consistency by adding less or more water.

● The dough reacts best to a warm (but not a hot) working environment. The dough itself is probably the best temperature gauge you have – it will become soft, sticky and moist in an over-heated room.

● Always work the dough on a cool surface.

KNEADING

Work the dough for at least ten minutes, slowly and rhythmically, pushing it away from you with the heels of your hands, then folding it back on itself. Turn the dough all the time – the more you knead it, the more pliable it becomes. In the end, its texture should be firm, malleable and elastic enough to stretch into a soft, slightly bouncy "rope" when stretched.

DECORATION

Surface decoration gives vital interest and texture to your model work. Always try to work with the dough directly on the baking sheet itself, otherwise you risk distorting the still soft model when you come to transfer it.

THE BASIC TOOLS

The tools and materials needed for the individual projects are listed, along with their step-by-step instructions, on the relevant pages, but you may find this checklist of the basic tools useful. You will find most of these modelling tools in your kitchen or around the house; any others will be easily obtainable at your local hardware shop. Some model work requires templates, and these you can cut from any pieces of scrap cardboard.

- Cardboard templates (see pp. 98-109)
- Non-stick baking sheet – a flat baking sheet without raised edges is best
- Ruler for measuring dough thickness. If it is lightly floured, a ruler also makes a convenient dough cutter
- Rolling pin
- Small kitchen knife
- Small wooden spatula, or any flat, paddle-shaped tool – for patting and smoothing edges and surfaces
- Small lid or jar of home-made dough paste – to stick layers of dough together
- Paintbrush for applying dough paste

YOU WILL ALSO NEED

The following items (pictured above) are used for certain of the projects.
- Pizza cutter – for cutting long strips of dough
- Lids to act as simple dough cutters
- Ovenproof bowls to use as moulds
- Pastry cutters of various shapes
- Pastry brush to moisten larger surfaces
- Tweezers for handling small beads
- Cotton buds for soaking up small areas of moisture, cleaning mirrors, etc
- Wire (1mm) for loops and threading
- Thin fuse wire for decoration
- Wire cutters
- Round-ended pliers
- Small mirrors
- Cork tiles for backing
- Self-adhesive or plain felt for backing
- Glue – the stronger, the better
- Wood (see pp. 78-81)
- Aluminium foil for moulded objects
- Decorative bits and pieces, such as loose beads from broken brooches, necklaces and earrings, buttons, and so on
- Dried cloves, also for decoration

STORING TIPS

- Take as much dough as you need for the project in hand and then seal the remainder in plastic food wrap (or place it in an airtight container) and store it in the refrigerator.

- When you are ready to use it, bring the stored dough back to room temperature by kneading it.

- Dough becomes soggy quite quickly and it does not store well for more than a day, or sometimes two, at a time, so only make as much as you can reasonably use.

- When putting dough to one side to use for a project already under way, cover it with a dry tea towel.

- Use a damp cover only when the dough has dried out and needs moistening.

MODELLING BY HAND

First, make your dough up using the basic recipe given on page 8. Make only as much dough as you are likely to use in one baking session. To achieve consistently successful modelling results, make sure that you keep your hands as cool as possible. The dough must be kneaded to make it pliable, but the more you manipulate it while modelling the stickier and more unmanageable it is likely to become. So always keep some flour handy to dust your hands if the dough becomes difficult to work.

SHELLS

The type of cockle shells and screwshells you see being made below have been used to decorate the frame illustrated on pages

96-7. Once you have picked up the basic technique, you could always try improvising by making a wider range of sea creatures. Even complex creatures can be successfully modelled if you reduce the body shape to a series of simple components that give an impression of the subject.

LEAVES

Leaves and petals are popular forms of decoration and are used in many of the dough craft projects in this book, but the trick is to make them look as realistic as possible (*see opposite*). Instead of trying to produce precisely the same leaf or petal every time, vary their shapes and sizes and arrange them in a haphazard, natural-looking fashion. This style of decoration is used on pages 27, 54, 65 and 72.

TIPS

● Make smaller shells from small balls of dough, indented in the middle with the handle end of a paintbrush, and then pinched at both ends.

● Starfish are easily made with a pastry cutter, but you could model them by hand.

MAKING COCKLE SHELLS

1 Take an appropriately sized piece of dough, roll it into an even ball and and flatten it to make a fat disc.

2 Pinching one end between the thumb and forefinger of one hand, gently press the opposite end into a shell shape.

3 Use a small kitchen knife to make shallow cuts on the surface of the shell and then score around the edges.

MAKING COCHLEA ("SNAIL" OR "SCREWSHELLS")

1 Take a ball of dough and roll into a short sausage. The length of the sausage determines the shell's size.

2 Make sure the sausage is consistently thick, and then gently turn one end two or three times until it forms a spiral shape.

3 Use your finger to make a hole in the other end of the shell and then turn it upward to make a realistic shell shape.

LOOPING

A piece of wire embedded in a salt-dough base makes an effective hanging loop for lighter objects. Looping is also a good way of joining securely together individual free-standing dough pieces.

THREADING

Threading wire into dough models is a technique used often in the projects in this book. Use 1mm thick wire to make the holes in the objects to be threaded.

OTHER TECHNIQUES

There are a handful of other techniques, such as scoring, using dough paste and indenting, that add texture and interest to the surface of your dough models.

Scoring the surface of salt dough is a technique used throughout this book. Not only is it a good way of adding a touch of professionalism to your model, it also provides attractive contrast lines when you come to paint it. Using a small knife, press the blade gently into the surface of the dough. If you are worried about committing yourself to freehand scoring, draw lines in pencil first as a guide.

To attach relief work to a model, mix a small piece of raw dough with some water to make a loose paste (you could use plain water, but this paste gives a firmer finish). Using a small paintbrush, apply the paste sparingly on the underside of the leaf, shell or cut-out shape to be attached. Then paint a little dough paste on the base area and join the two pieces together.

Indenting the dough with a chopstick or the handle end of a small paintbrush produces shallow depressions that can be painted or used as sockets for decorative beads and small balls of salt dough.

Flattening and patting a model's edges and surfaces with a small wooden spatula (wetted slightly) gives a smooth finish. You can also use the paddle of the spatula to transfer small pieces of relief work to the dough base without distorting them.

Cut-outs are simply shapes made with pastry cutters. Over-moist dough will give you soggy results, so make sure that the consistency is right before you start to cut out your shapes.

MAKING LEAVES

1 Flatten a small piece of dough and then cut and trim the basic leaf shape using a small kitchen knife.

2 Smooth the edges of each leaf with a wet knife blade. Add veins by gently pressing the blade into the dough.

LOOPING

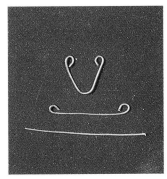

1 Cut a piece of 1mm wire about 2in (5cm) long. Using a pair of round-ended pliers, curve the wire and curl each end into an open O shape.

2 Using gentle and steady pressure, push the loop of wire into the dough base of the model until both curled ends are hidden from sight.

THREADING

1 Insert a length of wire through the object. As the dough starts to harden, turn the wire to prevent the hole closing up. Repeat this process until the object is cooked.

2 Using pliers, remove the wire, taking great care not to damage the dough, and re-thread it according to instructions given on the relevant projects.

BAKING

Salt-dough baking is not an exact science. Ovens differ and cooking times can vary according to the thickness of the dough being baked, the number of objects baked in the oven at the same time and the type of fuel used. By giving a standard ⅕in (5mm) thickness for dough bases – additional relief work should be about ⅛in (3mm thick) – it is possible to be a little more specific. The guide given here (*see right*) will give you an idea of approximate baking times.

For best results, preheat your oven at its lowest temperature and put your tray of dough on the middle shelf. Use the oven times given here as a general guide, but don't worry about being too exact – your own judgement should tell you whether an object is done, especially if you use the tap test (*see opposite*). When baking a mirrored object, however, you need to start with a cold oven to prevent the glass cracking.

TOOLS FOR BAKING
- Flat, non-stick baking sheets
- Long, flat-bladed knife or fish slice
- Oven glove
- Cooling rack

HALF-BAKING
Although this process can be fiddly, it is not at all complicated, but you do need to take care when handling half-baked dough.

APPROXIMATE BAKING TIMES

THINNER OBJECTS

Models ⅕in (5mm) thick:

(Cool oven) 3-4 hours
Gas Mark 2 – 300°F (150°C)

(Warming oven) 7 hours
Aga (oil) – 250°F (120°C)

THICKER OBJECTS

Models ⅕in (5mm) thick plus ⅛in (3mm) relief:

(Cool oven) 6-7 hours
Gas Mark 2 – 300°F (150°C)

(Warming oven) 10 hours
Aga (oil) – 250°F (120°C)

Faster times are possible with fan-assisted ovens.

For example, bake projects that have been moulded over crumpled aluminium foil or ovenproof bowls until they are just firm enough to handle without their shapes becoming distorted. Take the objects from the oven, shutting the oven door to retain the heat, and gently remove their moulds. Then return the salt dough models to the oven to harden off. This stage needs careful monitoring since the dough can easily overcook.

The length of baking gives you a great degree of control over the base colour of you model. Here you see examples of unbaked, half-baked and fully browned dough.

BROWNING

This baking technique gives different degrees of colour – from a pale gold to a deep brown – and it can be a very effective method for producing a natural finish and as a way of highlighting an object's shape. It can also give a deeper base colour, and this effects the appearance of the paint colour or the varnish used (*see pp. 14-15*).

After baking, return the salt dough to the oven and allow it to brown. Keep a close eye on this process, since over-cooking can make the dough very brittle and prone to cracking.

AIR-DRYING

This method is especially good for mirrors and picture frames (the bases are baked and the frames are attached later and then air-dried). Although it takes longer – days rather than hours – and therefore requires more patience, air-drying saves on fuel bills and doesn't monopolize the oven!

Again, exact drying times largely depend on the thickness of the model being produced and the ambient room temperature. Leave objects somewhere undisturbed on a flat surface in a dry place – an airing cupboard, for example, is ideal. The temperature should be constant, but you will still need to keep a close eye on the dough since it may start to warp slightly. On warm summer days, you can even dry thinner objects outside in the sunshine.

FILLING AND REPAIRING

Most cracks in dough models can be repaired easily, especially if you are vigilant and brush on some dough paste (diluted with extra water for hairline cracks) while the object is still warm. Heat is an excellent sealant and will aid the repair process.

Where the salt dough has been built up in layers, when using relief work, for example, any gaps and joins should be sealed and smoothed over by brushing on dough paste or water. After repairing, return the model to the oven. If you are still worried about the strength of a join, wait until the model is cool and use a little glue.

THE TAP TEST

● As the dough cooks, it begins to harden and the surface starts to look dry.

● When you think the dough is done, simply tap the object with your finger. If it sounds hollow, slide a long-bladed knife or fish slice underneath to loosen it from the backing sheet.

● Using an oven glove, turn the dough over and tap the base. A hard texture and a hollow sound tell you that the object is ready to be taken from the oven; a spongy texture and a dull, thudding noise mean it needs additional time in the oven.

PAINTING

If you can't commit yourself to a colour scheme straight away, make a rough drawing of the object and experiment on paper first. When you start painting the dough, be decisive. Watercolours dry quickly, so use bold brush strokes on larger areas, and apply the paint evenly. Don't over-fill the brush – the moisture could seep down into the dough.

Forget realism and be as dramatic as you dare. Rich, clashing colours are often far more effective than carefully matched shades. Try restricting yourself to a certain number of colours (the choice is yours), but keep a couple in reserve to create contrast between textures. Some objects lend themselves to groups of colours, but this need not be restricting. A sun plaque can be painted in shades of yellow, sand, brown, rust gold and burnt orange, for example. Use darker shades of the same colour for definition – a deeper green on the veins of leaves, for example.

For a stippled finish, dip a piece of crumpled paper towel or a piece of dry sponge into a small quantity of your chosen paint colour, and then dab at parts of the painted surface.

To create slivers of highlights, stroke gold paint on to the edges and rims of objects with a dry paintbrush, and then wipe over quickly with paper towel.

Blend colours with a cotton bud for a soft-edged finish to your work.

TOOLS FOR PAINTING

- Paints – tubes of watercolour are excellent for varying colour density and acrylic paints are good, too, but avoid oil-based products
- Paintbrushes – buy the best quality you can afford (four or five, ranging from a wide brush, for stroking on large areas of background colour, to a fine-haired brush, useful for small areas of fine detail)
- Paste brushes – cheap brushes are good enough to use for pasting, but ensure that bristles are firmly attached
- Gold paint
- Paper towel – for distressed effect
- Small pieces of sponge – useful to give a distressed paint effect
- Cotton buds – for blotting, smoothing and blending paint colours

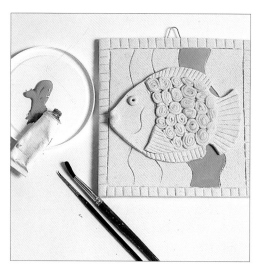

Dough models can be left in their natural, cooked colour. Some of them, however, come into their own only when they have been painted.

SAFETY

A dough model looks appealing. There is a real danger of children mistaking it for a cake or biscuit – this can be hazardous where a model contains wire or beads.

- Make sure that finished decorations and hanging plaques are kept well out of the reach of children.

- Keep lids securely on varnish tins when not in use and place sharp tools out of reach.

- Take sensible safety precautions at all times when baking.

each has received; and finally, always clean your brushes as soon as you finish working.

Egg white gives a natural-looking glaze for traditional and unpainted salt dough models, such as wreaths. Brush the egg white on before baking. This finish is not as long-lasting as chemical varnish.

TOOLS FOR VARNISHING
- Narrow paintbrush – about ½in (1.25cm) for general work
- Smaller brush – for fine detail
- Chopstick or wooden spoon handle, to stir varnish
- Polyurethane varnish (clear matt or gloss) – one small tin of each
- Turpentine – for cleaning brushes

VARNISHING

Not only does varnish help to seal and protect your work, it also adds a veneer of depth and richness to surface colours and brings out the natural tones of baked, but unpainted, salt dough. Careless varnishing, however, can ruin a beautifully painted object, so take your time!

Whether you use matt- or gloss-finish varnish is up to you. Some people prefer a high-definition shine on everything, while others go for a more subtle effect. Generally speaking, surface detail and decoration can be lost under too much shine, while simpler objects often look better with a gloss finish. If you don't intend to finish the back of an object with cork or felt, paint on a coat of varnish to seal it as soon as it is completely cool.

A few rules to bear in mind are: leave each coat to dry thoroughly before applying the next; each object will need five or six coats of varnish; when varnishing more than one object at a time, make a chart to record the number of coats

FINISHING YOUR WORK

Decorative finishes are largely a matter of taste. You may want to thread hanging plaques with ribbons, for example, or use beads and bells to cover threading wires.

Painting and varnishing the backs of finished pieces will protect your models, but if you are worried about filled cracks, general repairs or an uneven finish, you may prefer to cover the backs of plaques, frames, mirrors and some decorations.
- Use (thin) cork tiles as backing. Cut cork to size and glue it into place.
- Felt makes a good backing. Again, cut it to size and stick it in place.
- For a short cut, try sticky-backed felt – simply peel it back and stick it into place.

PRESERVING YOUR WORK

Although it is strong and long-lasting, salt dough is very susceptible to changes in temperature and to atmospheric damp. Varnishing your work will do a lot to improve its appearance as well as sealing and protecting it from harm.

Choose either a matt- or gloss-finish varnish, depending on taste, but don't apply the varnish until the dough is completely cool or the paint thoroughly dry.

TIPS

- Don't place salt dough in bathrooms or steamy kitchens – or in areas of a kitchen near steamy cookers and on work surfaces where a kettle is constantly in use.

- Never display salt dough models in rooms where the temperature fluctuates from being extremely hot to being extremely cold – a sunroom, storm porch or unheated conservatory, for example, since the dough may crack.

- Avoid placing salt dough too near radiators or heaters. Window ledges may seem ideal places to display your craft work, but they can become extremely cold and damp at night.

PLAQUES

1

2

3

4

MATERIALS

| Non-stick baking sheet |
| Ruler |
| Rolling pin |
| Small kitchen knife |
| Small wooden spatula |
| Small jar of dough paste |
| Paintbrush for dough paste |
| *Plus* |
| Cardboard template (*see pp. 98-109*) |
| 1mm wire about 4in (10cm) long |
| Wire cutters |
| Round-ended pliers |
| Small glass (to make central impression in sun) |
| Metal beads (or dried cloves) for eyes |
| Paintbrush |
| Varnish brush |

1 Working straight on to a baking tray, roll out the dough to a thickness of approximately ¼in (5mm), place the template on the dough and cut out the basic shape with a sharp kitchen knife. Carefully smooth any rough edges of the dough with a small spatula or barely damp paintbrush.

2 Using a ruler or knife, gently indent the dough diagonally, from point to point of the sun's rays, and outline the face by making a shallow, circular indentation using the rim of a small glass. Don't press down too hard.

3 To make the face, roll out two small sausage shapes for eyebrows, one and a half for the lips, a slightly thicker sausage of dough for the nose and two small balls to represent nostrils. Using the photograph of the finished sun shown opposite as a guide, position and attach all the pieces with dough paste. Press metal beads or cloves into position for the eyes (or use two small dough balls). The cheeks consist of two balls of dough, flattened to about ¾in (2cm) across. Score around the edges of the cheeks and attach them to the sun with a little dough paste.

4 Take a piece of wire and make a single loop at one end. Insert it into the centre top of the sun to a depth of about ¾in (2cm). Bend the other end of the wire into a hanging hook. Bake, paint and varnish.

FROWNING SUN

Although this design is very straight-forward, you should not feel that you have to re-create it exactly as it is illus-trated above. There is nothing to pre-vent you using the basic instructions for the sun plaque simply as the start-ing point for your own ideas.

You could, for example, experiment by adding threaded-dough cut-outs and beads, or any beads and trinkets you may have collected over the years.

You could also try using different paint techniques and colour schemes to create a more exotic-looking wall-hanging, one tailormade to fit in with the decoration in your own home. You could, of course, decide to turn the sun's frowning face into one with a beaming smile. The choice is yours.

The tricks to successful dough craft modelling lie first in thinking the pro-ject through thoroughly in advance, and then being prepared – so collect all the tools and materials you will need before starting. For the wire-threading technique used here, see pages 8-15, and you will find detailed bead instructions on pages 68-9.

HANGING HEARTS

This heart is a charming romantic symbol and very rewarding to make. Different paint effects can transform it into something elegant, dramatic or ethnic in minutes. Thread it with beads, bells or cut-outs and the result will be an original and personal hanging. Use the photographs as a guide, but don't be afraid to improvise.

If you want to vary the number and sizes of hearts, simply cut templates of your own, or buy some different-sized pastry cutters – tiny cutters are ideal for making dough beads, which you can paint in rich colours, patterns or designs. As long as you calculate the right amount of wire for threading the finished hanging, you can go on adding more and more decorations.

If this plaque is to be hung in a nursery or child's room, make sure that it is out of reach and the decorations can't be pulled off and swallowed.

MATERIALS
Non-stick baking sheet
Ruler
Rolling pin
Small kitchen knife
Small wooden spatula
Small jar of dough paste
Paintbrush for dough paste
Plus
Cardboard templates (*see pp. 98-109*) or pastry cutters
Wire cutters
Round-ended pliers
1mm wire about 6in (15cm), 5in (12cm) and 3in (8cm) long – if using templates supplied
1mm wire for final threading – see step 1 for length
Beads, bell, etc, for decoration
Paintbrush
Varnish brush

1 To calculate the length of wire for final threading, lay the cut-out dough hearts, templates or cutters on a flat surface, leaving the right amount of space for the beads or other decorations in between. Allow enough wire for bending into a hanging hook at the top and a loop at the bottom. Cut the wire and put it aside.

1

2

2 Working straight on to a baking tray, roll out the dough to a thickness of about ¼in (5mm), place the templates, or cutters, on the dough and cut around them with a sharp knife, or press down on the cutters, to make the heart shapes.

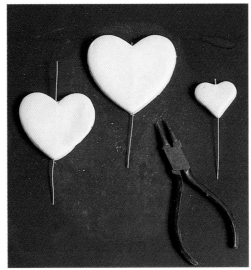

3 Taking care not to distort the dough by pressing too hard, smooth the flat surfaces and any rough edges with a spatula or damp paintbrush, and then carefully guide a length of wire down through the middle of each heart. Use the longest wire for the biggest heart and the shortest for the smallest, and so on.

3

4

4 Bake on the middle shelf of the oven, carefully turning the wires about every 15 minutes to prevent the holes closing up. When baked, allow the hearts to cool and use the round-ended pliers to withdraw the wires.

5 Paint and varnish the shapes and allow the hearts to dry thoroughly before proceeding.

6 Thread the beads, decorations and finished hearts on the wire. Shape the upper end into a hook and make a tight loop at the other end to support the hanging.

5

6

21

MATERIALS

Non-stick baking sheet	
Ruler	
Rolling pin	
Small kitchen knife	
Small wooden spatula	
Small jar of dough paste	
Paintbrush for dough paste	
Plus	
Cardboard templates (*see pp. 98-109*)	
1mm wire about 2in (5cm) long	
Wire cutters	
Round-ended pliers	
Paintbrush	
Varnish brush	

1

2

3

4

1 Working straight on to a baking tray, roll out the dough for the base to a thickness of about ¼in (5mm). With a sharp knife, carefully cut around the template shapes. Roll the dough for the smaller template pieces to a thickness of approximately ⅛in (3mm) and cut them out also. Position the smaller shapes on the base. Using dough paste and a damp brush, carefully stick and seal the shapes to the base. Take care not to press too hard or distort the model's shape when doing this. Tidy and smooth any rough edges.

2 Roll some spare dough into egg-shaped balls and arrange them in the basket. Stick them securely down with some dough paste (or water on a paintbrush). Roll a small ball to form the goose's eye and another, slightly larger, for her cheek. Position and stick them down.

3 Add the feather detailing, the apron frill and the textured weave on the egg basket by gently indenting the dough with a knife (*see pp. 8-15*). Take care not to cut through the dough or to distort its shape by pressing too hard.

4 To make the hanging loop in the middle of the top wing, curl each end of a piece of wire into an open O shape, using pliers or wire cutters to help bend and shape the wire. Bend the middle of the wire downward and carefully embed the curled ends into the dough until they are completely hidden, leaving just a neat loop or hanging hook on view. Bake, paint and varnish.

MOTHER GOOSE

Character plaques such as this lovable character make eye-catching details for a child's room. Mother Goose has been a firm favourite with young children for generations – and a hand-made plaque, modelled exclusively with a certain child in mind, adds a very special personal touch.

You will find all the templates for making a Mother Goose on pages 98-109. However, don't be deterred by the number of pieces involved. Once you have cut out all the shapes, the plaque itself is very straightforward to assemble. Take your time when tracing around and cutting out the templates from cardboard, since you can use well-prepared templates again and again. This may be extremely useful if you want to make two geese, perhaps painted in different colours, for a brother and sister, for example. You can also duplicate this plaque to make a series of flying geese to hang at different heights along a wall.

This is a decoration, not a toy. Take care to hang it out of the reach of smaller children.

PLAQUES

1 To calculate the length of wire, lay out the cow and moon templates with the correct space for the beads, stars and bell in between. Allow wire for a hook at the top and a bottom loop.

2 Working on a baking tray, roll the dough for the cow, moon and stars to a thickness of ¼in (5mm). Roll dough for the relief work pieces half this thickness. Cut the template shapes from the dough. Cut the stars with a pastry cutter and thread them with one of the 4in (10cm) lengths of wire.

3 Position the smaller pieces on the cow shape. Roll balls of dough for nostrils, and a sausage in between. Stick them all down. Squash and pierce the nostrils with the handle of a paintbrush. Use the same method for the eyes.

4 Insert wire for the cow's tail. Roll an olive pip-sized piece of dough and push it (half way) on to the end of the tail. Insert the 5in (13cm) length of wire through the cow's body.

5 Use a small glass or cutter to cut out the moon's cheek. Position it on the base, stick it down and score around the edges. Roll out a sausage and coil it for the eyebrow. Roll a dough ball for the eye (or use a metal bead) and position and stick it down. Insert the 10in (25cm) length of wire through the moon.

6 While baking, turn the wires (except for the cow's tail) regularly to prevent the holes closing. When cooled, withdraw the wires using pliers. After painting, varnishing and drying, thread the wire with the cow, moon, stars, beads, etc. Shape the upper end of the wire into a hook and make a loop at the other.

1

2

3

4

5

6

THE COW JUMPED OVER THE MOON

The inspiration for this model is the children's nursery rhyme. Since the theme is not realistic, you can be outlandish with your paint, patterns and textures, or lengthen the wires and add more moons and cut-out shapes.

If you have been working your way through the crafts so far, your confidence and skill should be increasing with each attempt. This plaque is a combination of the relief work you practised on the Mother Goose (*see pp. 22-3*) and the threading techniques used for the hearts (*see pp. 20-1*).

The small beads and wires could be harmful to young children. Position the plaque high up, well out of reach, if it is hung in a child's room.

MATERIALS
Non-stick baking sheet
Ruler
Rolling pin
Small kitchen knife
Small wooden spatula
Small jar of dough paste
Paintbrush for dough paste
Plus
Cardboard template (*see pp. 98-109*)
Wire cutters
Round-ended pliers
1mm wire about 10in (25cm) for the moon, 5in (13cm) for the cow, and 4in (10cm) for the tail and stars – if using templates supplied
1mm wire for final threading – see step 1 for length
Beads, bell, etc, for decoration
Star-shaped pastry cutter
Small circular glass or cutter
Paintbrush
Varnish brush

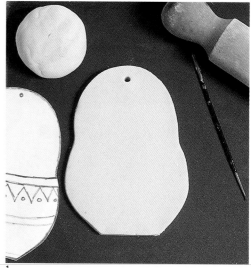

1

2

INTERMEDIATE LEVEL

VASE AND SUNFLOWERS

This attractive and extremely decorative plaque uses contrasting textures and vivid colours to make a big, bright impression. It is an ideal type of decoration for a kitchen, as long as the atmosphere there is not too damp – excessive moisture will soon cause the dough, even when sealed with varnish, to perish. You can always paint the sunflower vase to complement a colour scheme that already exists in the room, for example, or you could just as easily reproduce the patterns and colours of your favourite set of crockery?

Dried cloves add a natural texture to the middles of the sunflowers, but other spices, beads or small balls of painted salt dough make equally good alternative materials.

If you wish, you can finish off this sunflowers plaque by adding a cork or felt backing. Cut your backing to the correct size and shape and use a strong adhesive to stick the material into position. Otherwise, simply finish off the piece by varnishing the back of the dough as usual in order to seal it.

3

4

5

6

MATERIALS

Non-stick baking sheet

Ruler

Rolling pin

Small kitchen knife

Small wooden spatula

Small jar of dough paste

Paintbrush for dough paste

Plus

Cardboard template
(*see pp. 98-109*)

Cloves

Paintbrush

Varnish brush

Glue for cork or felt backing
(if desired)

1 Working straight on to a baking sheet, roll the dough for the base shape to a thickness of ¼in (5mm). Place the template on top of the dough and cut out the shape with a sharp knife. Using the handle end of a paintbrush, carefully pierce right through the dough to make a hanging hole in the middle of the top of the base.

2 Smooth the base, pat the edges with a spatula and check for any shape distortions. Roll a sausage from the dough, about ⅛in (1cm) wide, and run it across the middle of the base shape to make a lip for the bowl. Attach the lip with dough paste. Using a sharp knife, carefully score along the lip, making shallow indentations. Now add decorative zigzags to the bowl itself, using a sharp knife to again make shallow indentations in the dough.

3 Decide where to position your sunflowers (use the photograph of the finished project as a guide). Relief work should not be too thick – try to restrict yourself to about ⅛in (3mm) for the sunflowers and petals. Roll two balls of dough, flatten them slightly, and then position and stick them on to the base.

4 Model the sunflower petals by flattening and shaping them with your fingers. Bend the petals slightly to make them look more natural. Position and stick them down with dough paste and then lightly score them to add surface texture. Press cloves carefully into the middle of each sunflower.

5 Model the leaves in a way similar to the petals (*see also pp. 8-15*). Again, make the shapes irregular for a natural effect. Score veins on the surface of the leaves and don't neglect to score the edges, too. Arrange them as naturally as possible, and stick them down with dough paste.

6 Bake, allow to cool, and then paint. Use darker green to contrast the veins on the leaves and choose a bright, fresh and clear yellow for the sunflowers' petals. Contrasting colours make relief work more effective and three dimensional. Allow the paint to dry and then varnish. Glue cork or felt to the back (if desired).

MATERIALS

Non-stick baking sheet
Ruler
Rolling pin
Small kitchen knife
Small wooden spatula
Small jar of dough paste
Paintbrush for dough paste
Plus
Cardboard template (*see pp. 98-109*)
1mm wire about 2in (5cm) long for hanging loop
Wire cutters
Round-ended pliers
Paintbrush
Varnish brush
Glue for cork or felt backing (if desired)

FISH TILE

You can model this fish tile plaque relatively quickly – the skill lies in applying the surface texture and colour. Scoring techniques are used to give the impression of a border, or frame, around the plaque itself, and relief work adds further interest and depth.

In order to make the plaque look as impressive and as professional as possible, cut the dough very carefully and then smooth the edges. It is sometimes tempting to press too hard when you are working on a relatively large and simple shape, so keep an eye out for any distortion and make sure that your scored cuts or indentations are evenly applied to an equal depth.

To convey the feeling of deep, shimmering sea water and slippery fish scales, and to introduce some drama into the decorative scheme, use rich, marine shades and seaweed colours. This plaque uses contrasting colours for the fish. Gold paint was added as a highlight around the border and for the detailing on the fish's scales, eye and lips. For more information on painting techniques, see pages 8-15.

FISH TILE

1

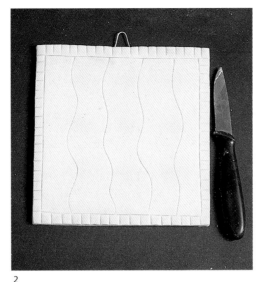

2

3

4

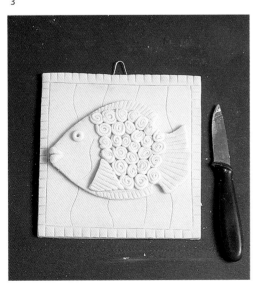

5

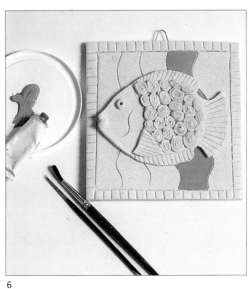

6

1 Working straight on to a baking sheet, roll the dough about ¼in (5mm) thick. Using a ruler and knife, cut a square about 6 x 6in (16 x 16cm). Smooth the edges and surface with a spatula. Make a hanging loop by bending the wire downward and curling both ends into open O shapes. Embed the ends carefully in the middle of the top of the base.

2 Score the border about ⅓in (1cm) in from edge of the tile right around the square. Make the decorative edging using small knife cuts. Now score wavy lines down the tile for the background effect. If you are worried about making these, lightly draw them in pencil first, which can be smoothed away. Cover the work with a dry towel to prevent it drying out.

3 For the fish, roll the dough out about ⅛in (3mm) thick. Using a template as a guide, cut out the fish and smooth its edges. Attach it to the tile with dough paste. Roll two small dough balls for the mouth and squash them slightly when sticking them down. Roll a tiny ball of dough, stick it down and pierce it with the end of a paintbrush to make the eye.

4 To create the body texture, roll out thin sausages of dough. Prepare the fish's body by brushing it with watery dough paste. Don't over-wet the dough. Curl the sausages and attach them and cut out a fin shape and attach.

5 Add texture to the fins and tail by scoring them very carefully. Check that everything is smooth and that gaps between the layers are sealed. Bake and allow to cool.

6 Paint and varnish. Finish the back of your plaque by attaching cork or felt, if desired.

29

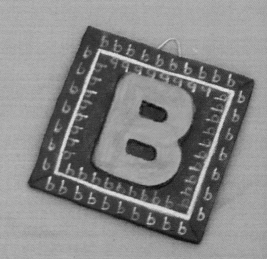

MATERIALS
Non-stick baking sheet
Ruler
Rolling pin
Small kitchen knife
Small wooden spatula
Small jar of dough paste
Paintbrush for dough paste
Plus
Cardboard template (*see opposite*)
1mm wire about 2in (5cm) long
Wire cutters
Round-ended pliers
Paintbrush
Varnish brush

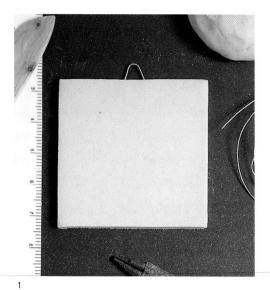

1

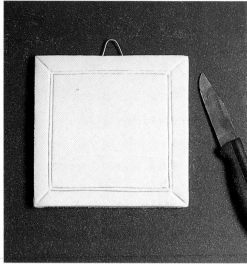

2

1 Working on a baking sheet, roll the dough out about ¼in (5mm) thick. With a ruler and knife, cut a square 4 x 4in (10 x 10cm). Smooth all over with a spatula, checking for shape distortions. Make a hanging loop by bending the wire downward and curling the ends into open O shapes. Embed the ends in the middle of the top of the base.

2 Score a line ⅓in (1cm) in from the edge of the tile and score a second line, 1mm in from the first to form a double border. Score diagonal lines from the corners to the borders. Cover the dough and set it aside.

3 To make the capital letter, roll the dough out about ⅛in (3mm) thick. Lay the template on the dough and cut around it. Use a flat surface (a ruler or the spatula blade) to transfer the letter carefully to the tile. Position it in the middle and stick it down using a small amount of dough paste.

4 Bake and allow the tile to cool thoroughly. Paint the capital and decorate the borders with lower-case versions of the letter in gold-coloured paint.

3

4

INTERMEDIATE LEVEL

ALPHABET TILES

These alphabet tiles can be as complicated or as simple as you want to make them. Inspired by the shapes of the initials themselves, this design uses the angles and lines of the capital and lower-case letters as natural surface patterns. Although you could score your own letters straight into the dough, the capitals are used in relief to add depth. Use the templates and follow the instructions above.

If the idea of making all the letters is too daunting, one tile decorated with the recipient's initial is an original gift idea – or you could double the size of the components for a larger plaque.

Making the alphabet isn't difficult. The basic design is the same for every tile – a capital and smaller letters with a decorative border – so there is plenty of scope for imaginative paint effects! Tiles painted in bright, primary colours could become teaching aids if hung on a child's wall, while gold, bronze and subtle shades have a more adult appeal. Take your time cutting the templates because, once cut, you can use them time and time again.

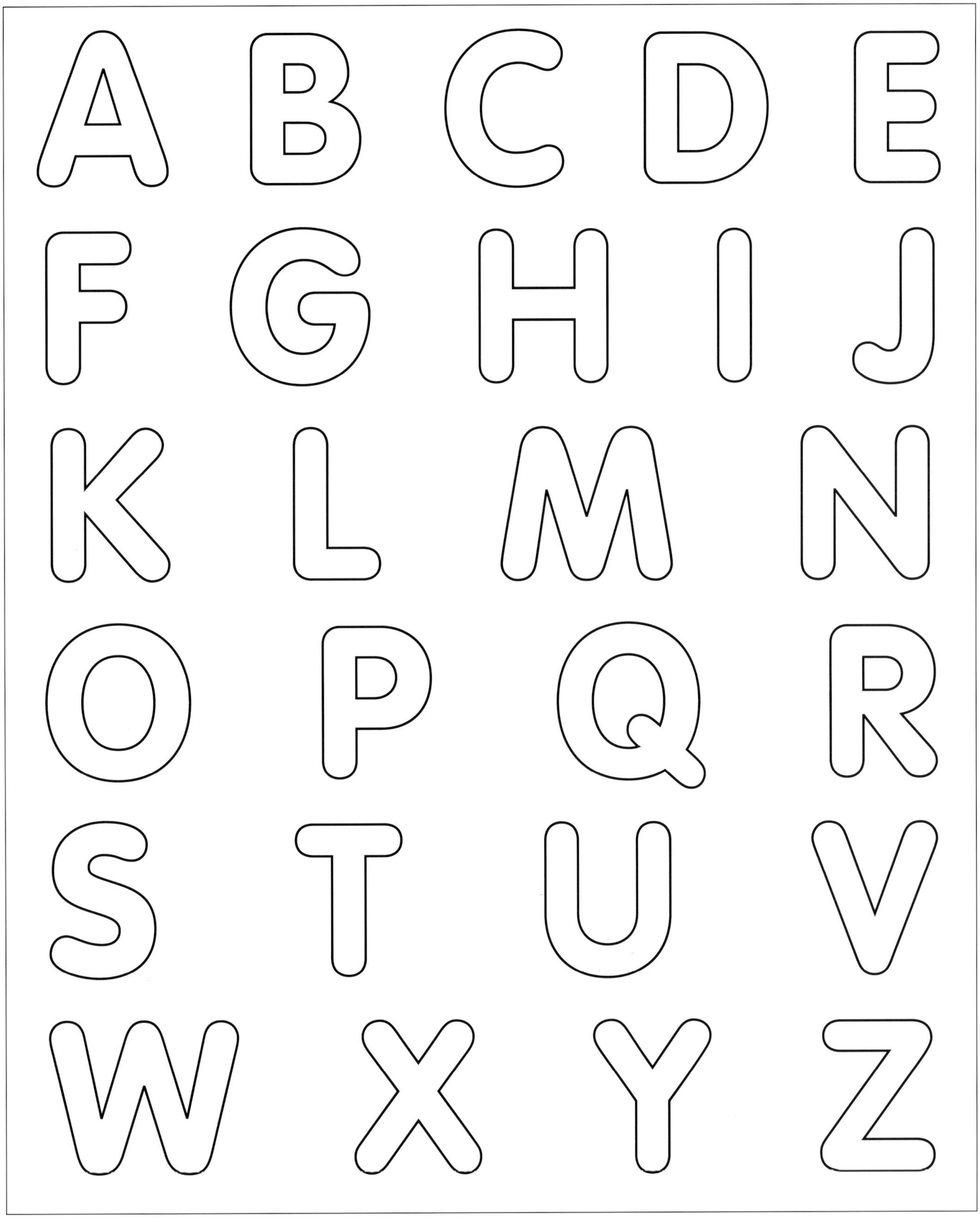

A B C D E

F G H I J

K L M N

O P Q R

S T U V

W X Y Z

PLAQUES

1 Working straight on to a baking sheet, roll the dough out about ¼in (5mm) thick. Using the cutter, press out the heart and smooth all over with a spatula. Make a hanging loop by bending the wire downward and curling both ends into open O shapes. Embed the curled ends carefully in the middle of the top of the heart, leaving about 2in (5cm) protruding to create a hanging loop. Cover the dough and put it aside.

2 Make a mould by shaping the foil into a hollow pocket about 3 x 3½in (8 x 9cm) and ½in (1cm) thick. Roll the dough out to about ¼in (5mm) thick, lay it over mould and trim around the edges.

3 Roll a bead shape from any scraps of left-over dough from the above steps.

4 Bake the heart-shaped, moulded dough pocket and bead side by side in the oven. While it is still warm (but not too hot to handle), remove the foil very gently from the pocket and place the pocket on the heart-shaped base.

5 Taking advantage of the fact that both pieces are warm, join them together (using thick dough paste to close any gaps). Use the dough paste to attach the still-warm bead. Return the assembled plaque to the oven and keep a eye on it while the paste hardens and seals the pieces. This should take about 15-20 minutes. Don't allow the dough to become brittle through over cooking.

6 Allow the dough to cool. If you are in any doubt about the pieces sealing firmly, use glue for a stronger finish (see pp. 8-15). Paint and varnish the model and fix cork or felt backing, if required.

1

2

3

4

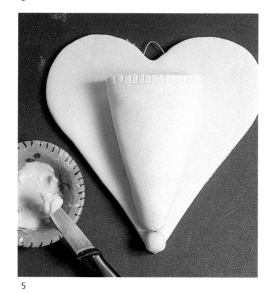

5

6

MATERIALS

Non-stick baking sheet

Ruler

Rolling pin

Small kitchen knife

Small wooden spatula

Small jar of dough paste

Paintbrush for dough paste

Plus

Cardboard template (*see pp. 98-109*) or pastry cutter

Aluminium foil

1mm wire about 3in (7cm) long for hanging loop

Wire cutters

Round-nosed pliers

Paintbrush

Varnish brush

Glue and cork or felt for backing (if desired)

ADVANCED LEVEL

HEART CONTAINER

Echoes of folk art give an ethnic flavour to this container. The heart plaque is practical, too, since you can use it to hold dried flowers, chopsticks or lightweight kitchen implements.

The colours are the key to its success, so here's a chance to be daring with your choice of paints. Follow the basic modelling technique described here, and then the paint effects are up to you. You could use the ideas illustrated above, or take inspiration from any number of traditional sources.

The "pocket" is made by using a simple moulding technique, which you can easily adapt to make containers in many different shapes and sizes. If you would rather make a smaller heart, for example, simply reduce the size of the template, pocket and mould, and then follow the modelling and baking techniques opposite to create your own very individual design.

Because aluminium foil is so pliable, it is an ideal material for moulding – just scrunch it into any suitable shape and then cover it with dough.

WHITE RABBIT

When it comes to making children's dough plaques, this classic character is far too well known to ignore, and almost too popular to need any form of introduction. Because he has so much personality (without being at all over-cute or sentimental), the White Rabbit, inspired by the book *Alice in Wonderland*, makes a perfect hanging plaque for children of all ages.

However, don't let the fact that he appears in the advanced section put you off – the rabbit is a combination of a lot of the skills used earlier in this chapter and, apart from some careful paintwork, there are no techniques used here that you have not already come across. The plaque is made up of different templates, placed on a rabbit-shaped base, and built up in relief. Don't forget to cover any pieces of dough that are not in immediate use with a dry towel.

It is the detailing that makes this plaque really special – everything, from the watch and chain to his wire spectacles, contributes to the overall effect. Work steadily and don't be tempted to rush the process or to cut corners, since the end result relies on careful craftwork.

This plaque is not a toy. If you use the rabbit as a hanging in a young child's bedroom, place it high up safely out of reach.

MATERIALS

Non-stick baking sheet
Ruler
Rolling pin
Small kitchen knife
Small wooden spatula
Small jar of dough paste
Paintbrush for dough paste
Plus
Cardboard template (*see pp. 98-109*)
1mm wire about 2⅜in (6cm) long for hanging loop
About 2⅜in (6cm) of thin, pliable fuse wire (for spectacles)
Toy eyes (from a craft store) or two metal beads
Wire cutters
Round-ended pliers
Paintbrushes (including fine brush for detail)
Varnish brush
Glue for cork or felt backing (if desired)

1 Working straight on to a baking sheet, roll the dough to a thickness of about ¼in (5mm). Using a template as a guide, cut out the basic shape and make a hanging loop from 1mm wire, bending the wire downward and curling both ends into open O shapes. Embed the curled ends carefully in the middle of the top (between the ears). Roll the rest of the dough to a thickness of about ⅛in (3mm) and cut carefully around the other templates.

2 Carefully lay each shape on to the rabbit's base, smoothing rough edges as you go, and use dough paste to stick them neatly into position. Check there are no gaps between the layers and that the rabbit figure is built-up and shaped as neatly as possible. Make the ear indentations and cover the dough to prevent it drying out.

3 To make the bow, roll a long sausage of dough about 5in (12cm). Flatten it unevenly and shape it into a horizontal "figure-8". Add a blob of dough for the central knot. Roll two more sausages, just over 1in (3cm) long, for the bow-tails and cut Vs into the ends with a knife.

4 Use a small spatula or flat blade to carefully lift the bow on to the rabbit, and attach it with dough paste.

5 To make the watch, roll a ball of dough and flatten it roughly into the shape and size of a small coin. Stick it on to the rabbit and add two tiny balls of dough to represent the watch's winding mechanism.

6 Roll a thin sausage about 2in (5cm) long for the watch chain. Attach one end to the watch and drape the rest across

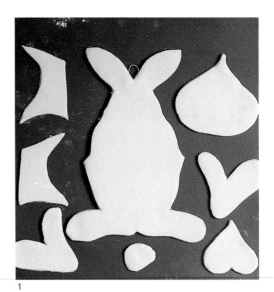

1

2

3

4

5

6

7

8

9

the rabbit's body, sticking it carefully down. Now score a line just inside the circular watch face for the casing. To make the eyes, use either toy eyes or beads. Use the eyes to indent the dough and put them to one side and stick them on after baking, or they may melt. Metal beads can be positioned and stuck on the model before baking, or you could roll small balls of dough to make the eyes and then paint them later.

7 To make the spectacles, use thin fuse wire. Make a wide, double-loop shape and push the straight ends into position, so that they rest naturally above the rabbit's nose.

8 To make the teeth, roll a small, fat sausage of dough about ½in (1cm) long. Score down its middle with a sharp knife. The finished result should look like a coffee bean. Stick it into position.

9 To add texture, use a sharp knife to score in whiskers, hair, eyebrows and paws. Try to make the surface texture look as natural as possible. Bake the model and allow it to cool, and then fill any cracks or gaps with dough paste. Paint it with a fine-haired brush, adding extra details to the watch, jacket and so on. Finally, varnish the piece and add a backing if desired.

BOWLS
AND POTS

1 Cover an ovenproof bowl with aluminium foil, taking care to smooth the surface and to tuck the ends over the edge of the bowl – about 2in (5cm) of the foil should overlap inside the bowl.

2 Roll the dough out to a thickness of about ¼in (5mm). Try to roll it into a rough circle, large enough to cover the bowl. Carefully place the dough over the foil-covered bowl. Trim off any excess from the edges with a sharp knife, taking care not to cut or tear the foil.

3 Smooth the surface of the dough with a damp (not wet) pastry brush, taking care not to stretch or distort the dough as you do so. Trim and smooth the dough, using a spatula to pat and flatten any rough edges.

4 When you are satisfied that the edges and surface of the bowl are smooth, turn it over and make the sun's rays by cutting V shapes into the dough with a sharp knife. If you are not confident enough to cut the dough directly, make very light guidelines with your knife first. Smooth any rough edges, taking care not to bend the sun's rays as you do so. Place the bowl upside down on the baking sheet and bake.

5 When the dough is hard to the touch, and solid enough not to distort, take it from the oven. Carefully remove the ovenproof bowl, and then peel the aluminium foil away from the inside of your dough bowl.

6 Replace the bowl, now the right way up, on the baking sheet and return it to the oven to finish baking. When the dough is cool, paint and varnish.

SUN BOWL

This sun bowl is very straightforward to make – and if you take plenty of time to cut, trim and finish the edges well, then the result should look extremely professional.

Air-drying dough is an option to baking. To do this, you need to dry the dough on its mould until it is hard enough not to distort, and then remove the mould and stand the dough bowl the right way up to finish drying.

No matter which technique you use, you will get better results if you roll the dough out to an even thickness – this makes it much easier to cut the sunray effect and its also prevents the overall shape distorting.

You can alter the design by using your own paint effects, colours and finishes, or by making the base colour of the bowl darker by browning it off in the oven – but keep a careful eye on the dough since it can easily become brittle if it is left in the oven too long. Varying the base colour gives paint effects an unpredictable and unusual character, so a certain degree of experimentation is called for.

1

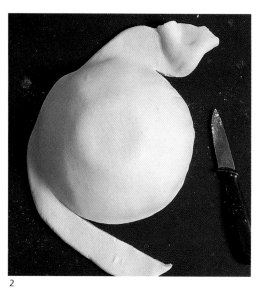

2

3

4

5

6

MATERIALS
Non-stick baking sheet
Ruler
Rolling pin
Small kitchen knife
Small wooden spatula
Small jar of dough paste
Paintbrush for dough paste
Pastry brush
Plus
Aluminium foil
Ovenproof bowl
Paintbrush
Varnish brush

BOWLS AND POTS

1 Cover an ovenproof bowl with foil, taking care to smooth the surface and to tuck the ends over the edge of the bowl – about 2in (5cm) of the foil should overlap the inside of the bowl.

2 Roll the dough out to a thickness of about ⅜in (1cm). Carefully place the dough over the foil-covered bowl. Trim any excess from the edges with a sharp knife, taking care not to cut into the foil.

3 Now smooth the surface of the dough with a damp (not wet) pastry brush. Trim and smooth the dough, using a spatula to pat and flatten any rough edges. When the edges and surface of the bowl are smooth, turn it over and cut a wavy line around the rim, taking care not to cut into the foil. Smooth any rough edges with a spatula.

4 Add exterior details by scoring lines around the bowl, about ⅛in (3mm) apart, and ⅝in (1.5cm) down from the rim. Follow the wavy line of the bowl's rim, using the photograph of the finished project as a guide. Score lines around the rim of the pot and between alternate lines. Place the pot upside down on the baking sheet and bake.

5 When the dough is hard to the touch, take it from the oven. Carefully remove the ovenproof bowl, and then peel the foil away from the inside of your dough bowl. Replace the bowl, now the right way up, on the baking sheet and return it to the oven to finish baking.

6 Remove it from the oven when cooked, and when it is completely cool, paint and varnish.

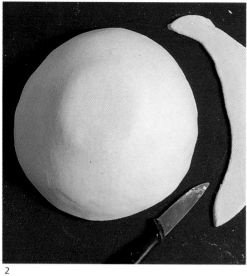

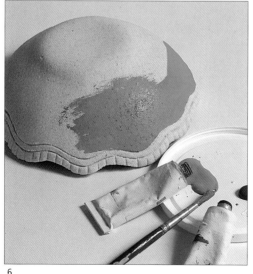

1
2
3
4
5
6

MATERIALS

Non-stick baking sheet
Rolling pin
Small kitchen knife
Small wooden spatula
Small jar of dough paste
Paintbrush for dough paste
Pastry brush
Plus
Aluminium foil
Ovenproof bowl
Paintbrush
Varnish brush
Sponge or paper towel

EASY LEVEL

SCALLOP-EDGED BOWL

A different bowl to the last project, but this one uses a similar technique and almost exactly the same modelling and baking method. The differences lie in the paint effects and the exterior scoring, which you can elaborate on, according to your taste.

If this is the first time you have worked with a mould, avoid extremes. The bowls used here are about 5-6in (13-15cm) across. There is no reason why you shouldn't make a larger bowl, but it is better to start on something manageable and fun and which has an excellent chance of success!

Refer to the chapter on materials and techniques (*see pp. 8-15*) for more ideas on finishes or stick to the colours used here. If you are not absolutely certain about the type of finish you want, then it's a good idea to bake a practice tile of dough with your pot and use it to experiment with colours. If the thought of scoring the bowl worries you, practise on an uncooked piece of dough until you feel confident pressing patterns into the surface.

MATERIALS

Non-stick baking sheet

Rolling pin

Small kitchen knife

Small wooden spatula

Small jar of dough paste

Paintbrush for dough paste

Pastry brush

Plus

Pastry cutters

Aluminium foil

Wire about 2in (5cm) long

Ovenproof bowl

Paintbrush

Varnish brush

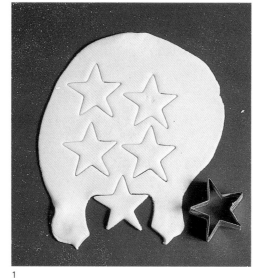

1

2

STAR POT AND LID

This star pot uses a modelling method similar to that for the previous sun and scalloped bowls, but includes a lid and cut-outs as decorative relief work.

You can choose any size base by using an appropriate ovenproof bowl as a mould, but note carefully the instructions for cutting the lid to ensure it is the right size for a good fit!

The shapes here are made with star-shaped pastry cutters, but use other shapes if you wish. If you don't have pastry cutters, make your own free-hand cut-out moons or geometric shapes, or have a look through the templates at the back of the book for alternatives (*see pp. 98-109*).

Make sure that the shapes are securely attached. Use dough paste to stick and seal the edges of the shapes and make sure that both the rim of the pot and the edges of the lid are neatly finished by carefully smoothing them before baking.

Rather than bake the pot on its own, it makes good, economical sense to save up a few craft items and then bake them all at the same time.

4

5

6

3

1 Cover an ovenproof bowl with foil. Smooth the surface and tuck the ends over the edge of the bowl – about 2in (5cm) of the foil should overlap inside the bowl (*see p. 44*). Roll the dough out to a thickness of about ¼in (5mm). Carefully place the dough over the foil-covered bowl. Trim off any excess from the edges with a sharp knife. Smooth the surface of the dough with a damp (not wet) pastry brush, and use a spatula to pat and flatten any rough edges. Now turn it over and start to add exterior details. Roll another piece of dough to a thickness of ⅛in (3mm) and press out as many star shapes as necessary, depending on the size of your pot.

2 Attach cut-outs to the exterior of the bowl with dough paste. if you want to add more texture, score the stars from point to point and add detailing around rim. Place your pot upside down on a baking sheet and bake. When the dough is hard to the touch, carefully remove the ovenproof bowl and peel the foil away from the inside of your dough. Return to the oven to finish baking.

3 To make the lid, roll the dough to thickness of ¼in (5mm). Place the cooled pot upside down on the dough and carefully cut around the rim to make a lid shape. Smooth the edges of the lid before baking.

4 Roll a small bead of dough. Push one end of the length of wire half-way into the bead and embed the other end into a dome-shaped foil base. Bake the lid and bead on the same baking sheet.

5 Attach the bead to the lid with dough paste if it is still warm enough to bond, or use glue.

6 When the bowl is completely cool, paint and varnish both the pot and the lid.

Non-stick baking sheet

Ruler

Rolling pin

Small kitchen knife

Small wooden spatula

Small jar of dough paste

Paintbrush for dough paste

Pastry brush

Plus

Small, washed, unridged tin
can – lips and ends removed

Star-shaped pastry cutter

Glue

Paintbrushes – including small
brush for face detail on lid

Varnish brush

SUN POT

This pot looks at its best when its colours are designed to co-ordinate with the scheme in the room in which it will be displayed. Here, the combination of its simple body shape and rich colour is emphasized by a shiny surface – if this is what you want, use gloss rather than matt varnish. You can vary the body by using different sizes of tin can, but take care since the edges of the can may be sharp.

The sun pot is a little more difficult to make than previous projects in this chapter, but only because the technique is slightly different. Wrapping the dough around a tube-shaped mould so that it is in exactly the right position to slide the mould out again takes care and patience, but no exceptional skill.

Take your time when attaching and joining dough pieces – the neater and stronger the joins, the better the finished results. An important tip is to make sure that your dough is rolled out to an even thickness – this makes the baking process far easier and the finished product more professional.

1

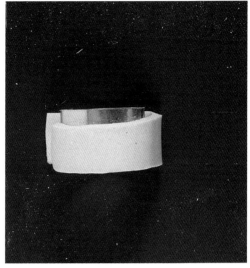

2

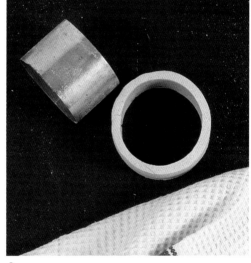

3

4

5

6

1 Roll the dough out to a thickness of about ¼in (5mm). Cut a strip of dough slightly narrower than the tin can itself.

2 Wrap the dough around the tin. A little of the tin should stick out above the dough so you can manoeuvre the tin out of the dough later on. The other end of the dough should be in line with the base of the tin. Strengthen the seam joining both ends of dough by rolling a sausage of dough, laying it along the join and flattening and smoothing it neatly down. When done, bake.

3 When the exterior is hard enough not to distort, gently remove the tin mould. Mend any cracks while the dough is still warm

4 Now roll more dough to a thickness of ¼in (5mm) and cut around the partly cooked dough tube to make a base shape. Repeat this process to make the lid. Roll out more dough to a thickness of about ½in (1cm) and cut star shapes using a pastry cutter.

5 Place the dough tube on to the cut base and seal and attach it inside and out using dough paste and a small brush. Smooth and neaten all uneven edges.

6 Bake the pot and lid until the base and inside of the pot are cooked and sealed, and the lid is baked. Attach a star to the lid using glue. When it is thoroughly cool, paint and varnish the pot and paint a sun face on the lid.

1 Cover an ovenproof bowl with foil, folding and overlapping about 2in (5cm) of the foil over the lip. Flatten the foil until it is absolutely smooth all over. Roll the dough out to a thickness of approximately ¼in (5mm) and cut around your template to make the fish shape.

2 Lift the fish dough shape and carefully lay it over the upside-down, foil-covered bowl.

3 Centre the fish shape and smooth it with a damp (not wet) pastry brush, taking care not to stretch the dough out of shape as you do so. Pat and smooth any rough edges with a spatula.

4 Using a small kitchen knife, score the fin and tail details on fish, using even pressure and taking care not to cut too deeply into the dough. Bake it until the surface is dry-looking and hard enough to be moved without distorting.

5 Remove the ovenproof bowl and peel the foil away from the dough. Repair any cracks with plain water while the dough is still warm, or use dough paste. Place your fish-shaped dough dish, the right way up, on the baking sheet and return it to the oven to finish baking.

6 When the dough has cooked, remove it from the oven, wait for it to cool, and then apply paint and a varnish finish to seal it.

FISH DISH

Here is a chance to be as adventurous or conventional as you like. You can either make one dish to use as a table centrepiece, a kitchen decoration or a useful container for bread rolls or party appetizers, or make a whole set of dishes in various sizes simply by altering the sizes of the ovenproof bowls and templates used.

This fish dish uses a combination of the skills and techniques you have already seen in this chapter, such as scoring, cutting and using moulds. But this time, instead of covering your ovenproof mould with an unshaped piece of dough, a template is used for the fish outline. The cut dough is then draped over the mould to give the fish its concave bowl-like shape.

Once you have scored in the surface detail, you can next use baking and browning techniques in order to vary the base colour of your dish, leaving a natural-looking surface for a plain varnish finish. Alternatively, you could use marine colours – anything to highlight the surface texture and emphasize the lavish nature of the dish.

1

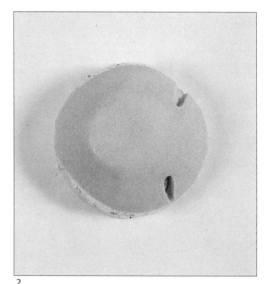

2

3

4

5

6

MATERIALS
Non-stick baking sheet
Rolling pin
Small kitchen knife
Small wooden spatula
Small jar of dough paste
Paintbrush for dough paste
Pastry brush
Plus
Cardboard template (*see pp. 98-109*)
Aluminium foil
Ovenproof bowl
Paintbrush
Varnish brush
Sponge or paper towel

LATTICE BOWL

The lattice bowl pictured here has simply been browned off in the oven and then varnished in order to emphasize the natural colour variations present in unevenly cooked dough. You could, however, spray your finished bowl with gold paint, or paint it in shades that match the decor in your home.

Although "bread" bowls and baskets are not all that original – people have been plaiting and weaving ordinary dough into decorative designs for many generations – when it is baked and varnished, the inherent preservative qualities of salt makes salt dough a much longer-lasting alternative.

This lattice bowl uses the same moulding technique as the other projects in this chapter. Since bowl sizes vary so greatly, it is almost impossible to calculate in advance exactly the right number of dough strips needed to create the effect. Cover any strips that are not immediately in use with a cloth, and prepare sufficient dough to roll out and cut when, or if, the original amount runs out.

Cutting flat ribbons of dough will produce a surprisingly delicate finish. As you become more skilled at weaving, you might try using even thinner strips. Rolling thicker dough sausages will give you a chunky, ethnic look, which can be very effective for larger everyday bowls – but bear in mind that thicker dough takes longer to bake.

1 For the first stage of making a lattice bowl (*see pp. 52-3 for a photograph of the finished project*), cover an ovenproof dish with foil. Roll the dough out to an even thickness of ¼in (5mm). Use a pizza cutter or a long knife to cut strips a little longer than the bowl. Start weaving your bowl by positioning a cross of two strips in the middle of the upside-down ovenproof bowl.

2 Now add more strips, weaving them over and under as you go. Make the gaps between your lattice-work as even as possible.

3 When the bowl is covered in woven strips, trim excess dough away from the rim. Gently squeeze the overlapping edging pieces so that they stick neatly together.

4 Roll and cut a strip of dough long enough to go right around the rim of the bowl. This should stay in place by itself, or paint on a little dough paste before attaching this edging strip if necessary.

5 Bake the bowl face down. Meanwhile, model enough dough-leaves to decorate the rim of the bowl (*see pp. 8-15 and 26-7*). When the bowl is hard enough to handle without distorting, take it from the oven, remove the oven-proof mould and peel away the foil. Arrange leaves around the rim, using dough paste to stick them on and to fill any uneven areas. Arrange the leaves to look as natural as possible, trailing and bending them over the bowl. Return the bowl to the oven until it and the leaves are baked. To deepen the natural colour, turn the oven up and keep a close eye on the dough as it darkens. When it is completely cool, varnish.

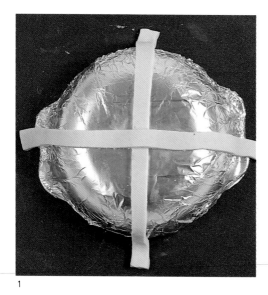

1

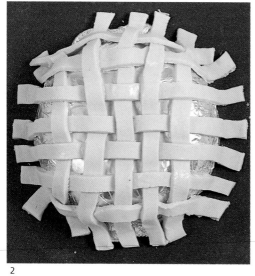

2

3

4

MATERIALS
Non-stick baking sheet
Rolling pin
Small kitchen knife
Small wooden spatula
Small jar of dough paste
Paintbrush for dough paste
Pastry brush
Plus
Pizza cutter
Aluminium foil
Ovenproof bowl
Paintbrush
Varnish brush

5

MATERIALS
Non-stick baking sheet
Ruler
Rolling pin
Small kitchen knife
Small wooden spatula
Small jar of dough paste
Paintbrush for dough paste
Pastry brush
Plus
Pizza cutter
Long kitchen knife
Aluminium foil
1mm wire
Wire cutters
Round-ended pliers
Small ovenproof bowl
Paintbrush
Varnish brush

ADVANCED LEVEL

POT AND STAND

Perfect for pot-pourri, seasonal spices or wrapped sweets, this pot has a real Eastern feel. The ovenproof bowl used here is about 3⅓in (8.5cm) across, so the lengths of wire, dough, etc, relate to this size. Rolling the dough to an even thickness and making rolled-up strips equal in length are vital when constructing the stand. If you have any doubts about the dimensions of the rolled strips, start again rather than waste time on an uneven finish.

Don't panic about hairline cracks, since you can mend these while the pot is still warm. But you could bake a few spare coils for the stand, just in case!

1

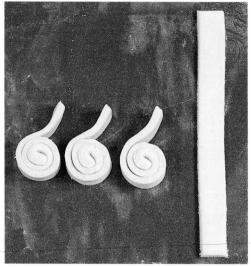

2

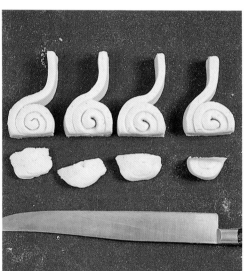

3

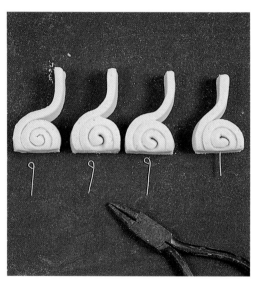

4

1 Roll out the dough to a thickness of about ⅕in (5mm). Using a long kitchen knife or a pizza cutter, cut four strips of dough, ¾in (2cm) wide and about 8in (20cm) long (suitable for the size pot illustrated in this project). Check that the strips are equal in both length and thickness.

2 Now roll the strips of dough into coiled legs, taking care to space them evenly in a straight line.

3 When you are sure that they are level, cut the ends off all of the coils in one slice using a long, sharp kitchen knife.

4 Using wire cutters, cut four pieces of 1mm wire. If using a bowl size of about 3⅓in (8.5cm), each piece of wire should be about ¾in (2cm) long. With the pliers, loop the wires at one end. Insert the looped ends into the ends of the coils, so that about ⅝in (1.5cm) of wire protrudes from each coil.

5 To make the pot, roll out the dough to a thickness of about ¾in (2cm). Cover your ovenproof dish with aluminium foil, smoothing it down all over and tucking the edges over the rim and overlapping the inside of the dish. Cover it with

dough and smooth it all over with a damp pastry brush or spatula. Using a sharp kitchen knife, cut the dough in line with the edge of the dish and smooth and even it with a spatula.

6 Now add the zigzag detailing to the dough pot and use the handle of a paintbrush to make indentations, being careful not to press down too hard.

7 Roll more dough to a thickness of about ⅕in (5mm). Using a large lid shape as a guide, cut a circle slightly larger than the pot to make the base. Mark a cross on the base,

5

6

dividing it into four sections. These marks will act as guidelines for positioning the coiled legs later.

8 Score a line about ⅜in (1cm) in from the edge of the circular base and carefully add knife detail all around the border.

9 Put the pot and base, and the coiled legs, into the oven for the first stage of baking. When the coils, base and pot are hard enough to be handled without their shapes distorting, carefully take the mould out of your dough pot and gently peel the aluminium foil away. Trim the wires back to approximately ¼in (5mm). Use the guidelines you made in step 7 on the circular base to position the coiled legs, and then attach them carefully by poking the protruding ends of the wires into the base. Use a small amount of dough paste to seal and smooth all gaps.

10 Secure the coils for baking by wrapping foil around them. This precaution will also help to keep them in place. Return them, attached to the base, to the oven until they are sealed and baked. At the same time, put the dough pot back in the oven to finish baking on the inside. Mend any hairline cracks in the dough while it is still warm. When the dough has thoroughly cooled, you can paint and then apply varnish to seal the finish.

7

8

9

10

DECORATIONS

FRIDGE MAGNETS

Hearts, flowers, stars, cats, fish, ducks and sheep motifs turned into fridge magnets all make perfect special gifts, stocking fillers or even charming and practical Christmas cracker surprises.

The technique couldn't be simpler, or faster – the artistry lies in using relief work, imagination and colour to transform the straightforward into something extraordinary.

The magnets pictured here could all made with pastry cutters and even children's craft cutters meant for play dough, but you could use your own freehand shapes or choose from some of the templates in the back of the book, reduced in size of course.

When it comes to painting the baked shapes, forget realism and choose bright colours and crazy patterns for maximum impact. Remember, these are fun objects, so enjoy yourself!

Metal cutters tend to make sharp, clean cuts in the dough, while plastic cutters have a duller, slightly more blunt finish. As long as you smooth off any rough edges, you should get good results from both types of implement.

MATERIALS

Non-stick baking sheet
Rolling pin
Small kitchen knife
Small wooden spatula
Small jar of dough paste
Paintbrush for dough paste
Plus
Cutters
Magnets (from craft stores and some hardware stores)
Paintbrush
Varnish brush
Strong adhesive

2

1

3

4

1 Gather together as many different cutters as you can. Remember that plastic cutters can be just as good as metal, as long as you smooth away any rough edges left on the dough. The more cutters you use the better, because spare dough shapes are bound to come in useful for practising different paint techniques.

2 Roll dough out to a thickness of about ¼in (5mm). Arrange your cutters so that they are close enough together to press as many shapes as possible out of one piece of dough, but far enough

apart to make a clean impression. Press out one shape at a time and cover the rest of the dough with a cloth to keep it moist.

3 Add surface texture, either by scoring or attaching relief work. The wool on this sheep, for example, is made from tiny balls of rolled dough, fixed to the base-shape cut-out with dough paste.

4 Even the simplest shapes can be transformed by adding a few eye-catching details. This square, scalloped cutter makes a good base shape for a flower. Roll

a dough ball, place it in the middle of the square base and indent the centre with the handle of a paint-brush. Model some petals (*see pp. 8-15*) of a suitable scale and then attach with dough paste to give a natural-looking effect. When the shapes have been baked and allowed time to cool thoroughly, paint and varnish them. Attach magnets to the backs of the cut-outs using one of the modern, instant-bonding strong adhesives.

EASY LEVEL

CHRISTMAS TREE DECORATIONS

These skill in making these Christmas tree decorations lies in trimming the cut-out shapes and mini-wreaths so that they look original. Paint your shapes in rich colours, making them shine through layers of glossy varnish, and then thread them with lengths of bright-coloured ribbon.

Burnished gold, deep reds, purples and greens are all effective colours to use for Christmas decorations. Try to make your paint effects contrast with the green of your tree. You could even add some sparkle by embedding glittering beads into the dough.

Although tree decorations are limited to a certain size (heavy ornaments pull on branches), the ideas here could lead to bigger things. Make your own templates to produce larger decorations, and use them to hang on picture hooks, for example, or from ceiling beams and doorways around the house.

Once painted and trimmed, smaller decorations can be used as special alternatives to bows on gift wrapping, or given in sets as presents in themselves.

1

2

3

4

1 To make the hearts, working straight on to the baking sheet, roll the dough out to a thickness of about ¼in (5mm). Using a heart-shaped cutter, press out as many shapes as possible from the piece of dough. With the handle end of a paintbrush, make a hanging hole in the top of each heart. Check that the holes are open by turning the end of the brush inside each hole until you can see the baking sheet underneath. Bake the hearts and when they are thoroughly cool, paint and varnish them and thread ribbon through the holes.

2 To make the stars, working straight on to the baking sheet, roll the dough out to a thickness of about ¼in (5mm). Using a star-shaped cutter, press out the shapes. Cut pieces of wire and loop them at one end. Embed the looped end into each star. The lengths of the wire depend on the size of the star cut-outs, but about 1¾-2in (4-5cm) of wire should be left protruding from one end. Bake the shapes and when they are cool, spray them with gold paint and varnish. Turn the wire at the top to form a hook, and then thread them with ribbon.

3 To make small wreaths, working straight on to the baking sheet, roll out sausages of dough – the thicknesses and lengths depend on the size preferred. Squeeze the ends together gently to form dough circles.

4 To make the oranges, roll small balls of dough, attach them to the wreaths and then push a dried clove into the middle of each ball. Make the leaves (*see pp. 8-15*) and arrange them around wreath to create a natural effect. Bake the shapes and when cool, paint and varnish them.

BEADS

Salt dough is the perfect medium for making decorative beads. Not only is it flexible enough to allow you to vary the sizes and shapes of the dough beads to suit the scale and style of the model you may be making, but if you bake them carefully, and then paint and varnish them, they are strong enough to last for a considerable period of time.

The step-by-step instructions and photographs on the following page should help you to avoid some of the more aggravating and time-wasting slip-ups that can frequently occur when working with these small and fiddly objects. One such example is threading sufficient wire through the middles of the beads to hold on to while you paint and varnish them in order to prevent them smudging.

If you prefer something more austere and understated, you could eschew painted effects altogether and opt for a natural look instead.

Try baking the beads for different lengths of time – the longer in the oven the deeper the shade of brown. Take care, however, since over-baking can lead to brittleness. When the beads have thoroughly cooled, simply varnish the end results. Experiment with different finishes of varnish, too. Gloss and matt types give different colour intensities in the underlying surface.

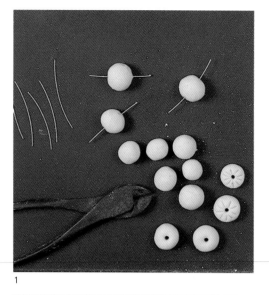

1

2

3

4

MATERIALS
Non-stick baking sheet
Ruler
Rolling pin
Small kitchen knife
Small wooden spatula
Small jar of dough paste
Paintbrush for dough paste
Plus
Pastry cutters
1mm wire
Wire cutters
Round-ended pliers
Paintbrush
Varnish brush

1 To make round beads, first roll balls of dough to the desired size and push a length of wire through each one. Wire lengths depend on the sizes of the beads, but as a rough guide, about 2in (5cm) of wire should protrude from either end of each bead.

2 Scrunch some aluminium foil into a firm dome shape. Use this as a base to stick the wired beads into as they bake. Allow them to bake and cool. Hold each bead by its wire while painting, then remove the wires with pliers and use holes for final threading.

3 To make star- and heart-shaped beads, working straight on to the baking tray, roll the dough to a thickness of about ¼in (5mm) and cut the shapes out using pastry cutters. Carefully push a length of wire through each shape, leaving 1-2in (2-5cm) protruding from either end. Allow them to bake and cool. Hold each shape by its wire while painting, and then remove the wires and use the holes for final threading.

4 Use rich colours to paint your beads – even the most abstract blobs and patches of colour can be extremely effective when applied with flair. A gloss-finish varnish will give additional depth and brilliance to any pattern you apply, and a shiny surface can add a jewel-like richness to surface coloration. A matt-surface finish, on the other hand, is useful when you want to suppress a colour or when your model is going to be very directly lit and you don't want it to throw too many reflections back into the room.

INTERMEDIATE LEVEL

VALENTINE CENTREPIECE

This splendid Valentine centrepiece is decorated in the rich, romantic colours that we traditionally associate with love, passion and, of course, St Valentine's Day. If, however, your tastes are more conservative and a little less flamboyant, you could always steer clear of the lush scarlet, purple and gold and use the paler, more pastel shades and silver instead.

Although this dish is not at all complicated to make, you should not attempt to hurry it. Take plenty of time to roll the dough out to an even thickness and join every section of the dish as neatly and firmly as possible.

The dish combines two well-tried techniques from other projects in the book – cut-out shapes and moulding. The size of the finished bowl depends on the sizes of the hearts you decide to use. If you have a good selection of smaller, heart-shaped cutters, you could try laying them on a smaller ovenproof bowl, or cut templates to an appropriate size. The shapes used here are ideal for an average-sized dish.

1 Cover an ovenproof bowl with foil, smooth the surface, and ensure that about 2in (5cm) of foil overlaps the inside of the bowl. Roll the dough out to a thickness of about ¼in (5mm). Cut out four large hearts and arrange them over the back of the bowl. Make sure they are all evenly spaced.

2 Seal the hearts together by rolling small dough sausages, placing them in between the hearts, and smoothing and joining the edges with dough paste.

3 Cut out four medium and four small hearts. Arrange the medium hearts to overlap the large. Join the medium and large hearts. Arrange the small hearts, using dough paste to attach them. Don't distort the dough shapes.

4 Score edging lines around the medium and small hearts. Roll sausages of dough, coil and attach them to the medium hearts with dough paste. Bake until the dough is hard enough to handle without distorting. Remove the ovenproof dish and peel away the foil. Return the bowl to the oven, the right way up, until baked. When cool, paint and varnish.

1

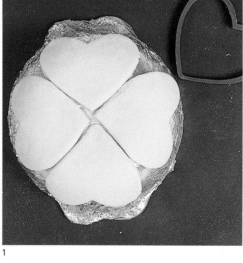
2

3

4

DECORATIONS

1 Working straight on to the baking sheet, roll a long sausage of dough about 22in (56cm) long and 1in (2.5cm) wide. Join the two ends together to make an even, oval shape.

2 Now flatten the oval with a rolling pin, taking care to make the dough the same thickness all over. If necessary trim off excess dough with a sharp knife. Smooth any rough edges with a spatula.

3 To make oranges, roll dough balls and embed dried cloves in their middles. Cover any dough not immediately in use to prevent it drying out.

4 Model the leaves (*see pp. 8-15*) and add veins by scoring inward from the edges to the middles. Attach the oranges and leaves with dough paste, taking care not to overwet the base shape or relief work. As always, cover any dough not immediately in use.

5 Carry on layering your leaves and oranges. Don't worry about making a symmetrical arrangement. Try instead to achieve a decorative and natural-looking composition.

6 Bake the wreath. and then return it to the oven to "brown off". Keep a careful eye on this process and remove your wreath as soon as it turns the right shade of brown. When the dough is completely cool, you can paint the wreath or simply apply varnish to seal it and bring out the dough's natural colour.

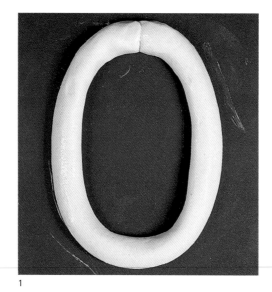

1

2

3

4

5

6

INTERMEDIATE LEVEL

ORANGE WREATH

Wreaths are the most traditional of dough crafts and can be used to decorate the home for such family occasions as Christmas, harvest festivals, Easter and Thanksgiving.

Most of this wreath is modelled by hand, using techniques covered in earlier projects (*see also pp. 8-15*). If you are not confident about moulding petals yourself, you could cut them out first, or use petal-shaped pastry cutters – although this would give a more manufactured, static impression than hand-crafted relief work.

The petals and oranges should look as lush as you can make them, so space them quite closely together. If you are making a large wreath, however, don't overload it with relief work – not only will it take far longer to bake, it may lose its shape when propped up.

The natural tones of baked dough make a real impact when "browned off" in the oven and varnished. You could paint the wreath in greens and oranges, but baked browns should provide more than enough depth of colour.

CANDLESTICKS

No matter how exclusive they may be, shop-bought candlesticks cannot match the originality and charm of home-made crafts.

Once you have followed the basic modelling instructions on the following pages, you can then proceed to paint and finish your candlestick with some very personal finishing touches. You can choose either to reproduce the colours as shown here, or to decorate your candlestick to match your table linen and crockery, for example.

Making a few candlesticks at a time is a sensible precaution – especially if you are at all nervous about the end result. Spare legs for the stand or an extra bowl could come in useful as replacement parts for defective pieces, or simply make more than one candlestick to decorate a festive table.

All the proportions for this craft relate to a 3⅓in (8.5cm) ovenproof bowl. You will probably find it easier to follow the instructions if you use a similar-sized bowl. If you want to make bigger or smaller candlesticks, however, then simply adjust the proportions accordingly.

The coiled legs are a very important element of this project. They provide a tripod arrangement for the decorative bowl and should make a secure and steady base. For this reason, roll out the dough to exactly the same lengths and widths for each leg.

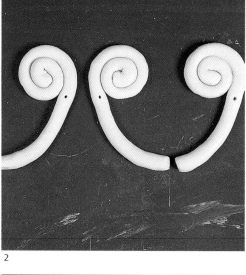

1

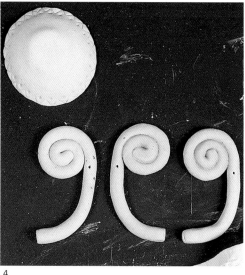

2

MATERIALS

Non-stick baking sheet
Ruler
Rolling pin
Small kitchen knife
Small wooden spatula
Small jar of dough paste
Paintbrush for dough paste
Pastry brush
Plus
Aluminium foil
1mm wire
Wire cutters
Round-ended pliers
Small ovenproof bowl
Paintbrush
Varnish brush

3

4

5

1 Working straight on to the baking tray, roll out three sausages of dough, each measuring about 10in (25cm) long and ⅜in (1cm) wide.

2 Curl the ends of the dough sausages, positioning them in a straight line on the baking tray. Doing this will make it easier to assess the lengths and ensure that they are equal. Using a piece of 1mm-thick wire, make a threading hole just below the coil of each leg. Check that the hole goes right the way through the legs by rotating the wire gently and slowly

6

7

8

9

until you can feel the baking tray underneath the dough.

3 Cover a small ovenproof dish with aluminium foil, making sure that the foil overlaps the rim of the bowl and tucks inside it by about 2in (5cm). Smooth the foil carefully all over. Roll the dough out to a thickness of ¼in (5mm) and place it over the foil-covered bowl. Trim off any excess dough, taking care not to cut into the foil.

4 Bake the bowl and legs together in the oven. When the dough bowl is hard enough to be handled without distorting its shape, remove the ovenproof bowl and peel away the foil. Return the bowl to the oven until it is cooked. Whether or not the legs are baked by this time will depend on their thickness as well as the type of oven you are using.

5 Remove the dough from the oven and when it is cool, paint the legs and bowl.

6 When the paint is dry, apply coats of varnish, but take care that you don't clog the threading holes in the legs.

7 When the varnish is completely dry, thread 1mm-thick wire through the holes in the coiled legs.

8 Manoeuvre the legs carefully into position to make a firm and even tripod arrangement.

9 Carry on wrapping the wire around the coiled legs until they are firmly and neatly secured.

BOOKENDS

Practical, decorative and very unusual – these bookends prove that salt dough is an extremely adaptable and versatile craft medium. Although this craft contains more elements than usual (see instructions on the following pages for the wooden stand), the sun shapes themselves are surprisingly simple to make. If you have already worked your way through some of the projects in the first chapter on plaques, then the sun faces should be nothing more than a logical extension of the cutting, relief work and scoring skills covered there.

Make sure that you roll the dough out to an even thickness and smooth the surfaces and edges to give a good, professional finish. Score the textured areas carefully and attach relief work as neatly as possible, but don't strive for perfection. Extra care is necessary because simplicity tends to highlight faults in technique, but you should avoid a "manufactured" look.

These suns in the example pictured here were sprayed with gold paint. "Browning off" in the oven can give a darker base colour, adding depth to the surface when it is sprayed.

Once you have read through the instructions, you can either copy this project exactly as here, or try a few variations of your own. Character bookends are perfect for a child's room, so why not incorporate the White Rabbit or Mother Goose in the first chapter section (*see pp. 22-3 and 36-9*), or cut out a simple moon shape. Brightly patterned hearts, stars and fish are good alternative motifs for slightly older children.

Remember to keep dough models away from damp. If, for example, you want to use the bookends for cookery books, make sure they are nowhere near kettles or stoves.

MATERIALS

| Non-stick baking sheet |
| Ruler |
| Rolling pin |
| Small kitchen knife |
| Small wooden spatula |
| Small jar of dough paste |
| Paintbrush for dough paste |
| Pastry brush |
| *Plus* |
| Cardboard template (*see pp. 98-109*) |
| Gold spray paint |
| Varnish brush |
| Cork tiles for backing |
| Strong adhesive for backing |

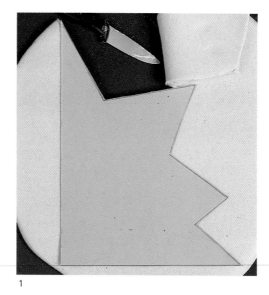

1

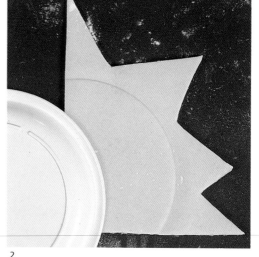

2

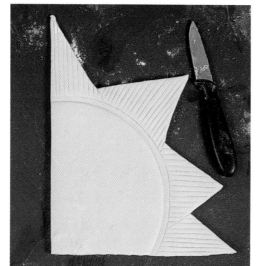

3

4

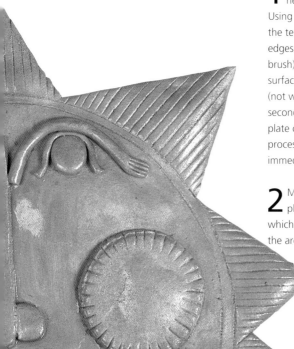

1 Roll the dough out to a thickness of about ¼in (5mm). Using a sharp knife, cut around the template. Smooth any rough edges with a spatula (or a damp brush). If necessary, smooth the surface of the dough with a moist (not wet) pastry brush. Make a second face by turning the template over and repeating the process. Cover any dough not immediately in use.

2 Mark the face's outline with a plate. If you are unsure about which size to use, practise making the arc shape on the template, rather than mark the dough incorrectly. Repeat this process for the second sun face, and then cover the dough with a cloth to keep it moist.

3 For each sun's face, score the sunrays. Using a knife, make a second internal arc following the outline of the first.

4 For the features of each sun's face, first roll a sausage of dough for the nose and flatten it out evenly. Then roll a small ball of dough and flatten it to make a nostril. Now roll a larger ball and flatten it to make the cheek and use a knife to add detail. Flatten a smaller ball for the eye and roll a thin sausage for the eyelid/brow. Attach the features with dough paste. Bake both faces. When they are cool, spray them with gold paint, wait for it to dry and varnish the backs and fronts. While the final coat of varnish is drying, cut around the original template to make sun shapes in cork. Attach cork to the backs of the faces with a strong adhesive. Finally, use a strong adhesive to attach the sun faces to the wooden backings you have already prepared (*see right*).

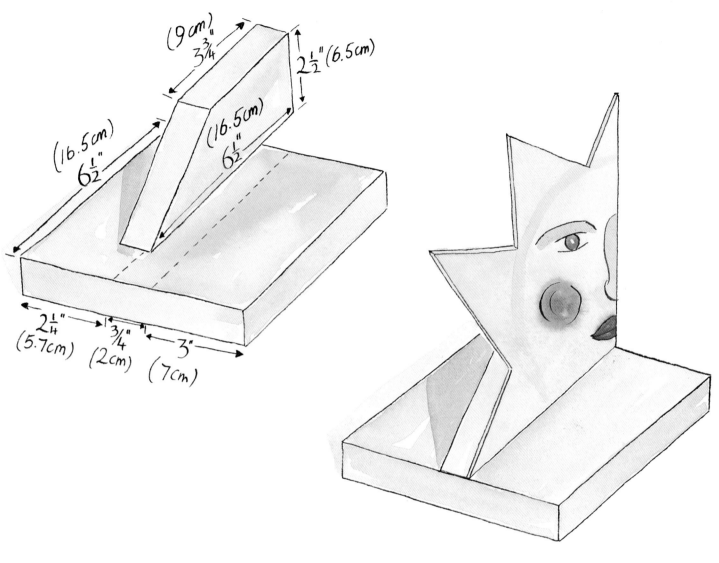

(9cm)
3¾"

2½" (6.5cm)

(16.5cm)

(16.5cm)
6½"

(16.5cm)
6½"

2¼"
(5.7cm)

¾"
(2cm)

3"
(7cm)

MAKING THE BOOKENDS

MATERIALS

2 blocks of ¾in (2cm) wood –
6½ x 6in (16.5 x 15.25cm) and
6½ x 2½in (16.5 x 6.5cm)

Ruler and pencil

Woodworking glue

Saw and T square

Screws and screwdriver

Strong adhesive

1 Using the larger of the two blocks of wood as the base for your bookend, measure 3in (7cm) in from the front edge and make a light pencil mark, and 2¼in (5.7cm) from the back edge and make a mark. Then, using a T square draw guidelines across the wood ¾in (2cm) apart. Next, use the bottom ray of the sun dough model as a guide, draw a line from the lower corner of the smaller block of wood. Saw the corner off.

2 Position the smaller block of wood between the lines you have drawn on the larger base

piece of wood. Make two drill holes, coming up through the bottom of the base and into the top piece. Separate the two pieces of wood, spread woodworking glue on the base, position the two together again and drive two screws firmly home. Make sure that the heads of the screws are below the surface of the wood. Finally, attach the sun model to its support using strong adhesive. Repeat this series of operations for your second bookend.

ADVANCED LEVEL

FISH WREATH

This project illustrates how a little ingenuity can turn the simplest of shapes into something stunning. At first, this wreath appears to be an odd-looking template with a keyhole centre. Once you start adding the elements illustrated opposite, however, the wreath takes shape and the end result is an exotic wall hanging with a classical feel.

Here is another opportunity for you to add your own ideas and preferences.

You may like to use the wreath as a festive hanging, rather than an all-year-round decoration – in which case, spraying it gold or silver may seem more appropriate. Reducing the size of the template will give you a smaller base to model on for Christmas tree or table decorations. However, the smaller the wreath, the more fiddly the relief work and, besides, there is something luxurious about the full-sized, richly coloured version.

Although the watery theme may tempt you to hang the wreath in a bathroom, only do this if you can be sure that the dough will not be exposed to steam and damp.

MATERIALS
Non-stick baking sheet
Rolling pin
Small kitchen knife
Small wooden spatula
Small jar of dough paste
Paintbrush for dough paste
Pastry brush
Plus
Cardboard template (*see pp. 98-109*)
Paintbrush
Varnish brush

1

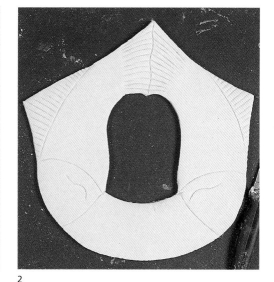

2

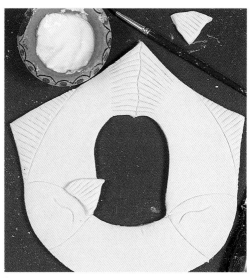

3

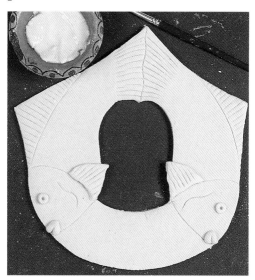

4

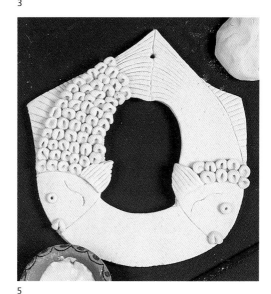

5

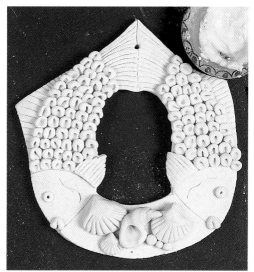

6

1 Working straight on to the baking tray, roll the dough to a thickness of about ¼in (5mm). Cut around the template carefully and smooth any rough surfaces and edges so that the dough base shape is as neat as possible.

2 Lightly score in the fish outlines with a knife, using the photograph as a guide.

3 Roll out the dough for the fin relief work to a thickness of about ⅛in (3mm). Cut out the fin shapes and attach them with dough paste, taking care not to overwet the dough pieces, and finish the edges neatly.

4 Roll out and curl small dough sausages for the lips. Roll dough balls for the eyes and stick them down with dough paste. Indent the centres slightly. Now add detailing to the fins using a sharp knife.

5 Make a hanging hole at the top of the wreath with the handle end of a paintbrush. Make sure that the hole is fully open by turning the end of the brush until you feel the baking tray underneath the dough. Roll small dough balls, attach them with dough paste and indent them with the paintbrush handle. Add line after line of these indented balls to form the fish's scales.

6 Model shells from dough (*see pp. 8-15*). and attach them to the wreath using dough paste. When all of the elements are assembled and securely fixed in position, place the wreath in the oven and bake. When it is thoroughly cool, paint and varnish.

MIRRORS
AND FRAMES

1 Roll the dough out to a thickness of about ⅜in (1cm). With a sharp knife, cut out a 6in (15cm) square. Smooth the edges of the square with a spatula and make sure that the surface of the dough is flat and even.

2 Position your mirror in the middle of the dough base and press down gently to embed it in the dough. Tap around the edges of the dough with a spatula to even up the square if necessary.

3 Roll out another piece of dough to a thickness of ¼in (5mm) and cut it into exactly the same size square as your base and mirror. Lay the new square on top and neatly seal the two layers of dough together by brushing dough paste around the edges.

4 Making sure that it is centred, place your pastry cutter on the top layer of the dough and press out a square, exposing the mirror underneath.

5 Seal any gaps around the mirror and frame with dough paste. Roll small sausages of dough and coil the ends.

6 Arrange the dough coils on your mirror frame and stick them down using dough paste. Clean any smudges of paste off the mirror surface with cotton buds. Bake, or air-dry, the mirror. If using an oven, put the mirror inside *before* turning it on. When it is baked, turn the oven off and allow it to cool down with the mirror still inside. When the dough is cool, paint and varnish it. Add a cork backing if desired.

1

2

3

4

5

6

MATERIALS

MATERIALS
Non-stick baking sheet
Ruler
Rolling pin
Small kitchen knife
Small wooden spatula
Small jar of dough paste
Paintbrush for dough paste
Pastry brush
Plus
Mirror – about 5in (12cm) square
Cotton buds for cleaning mirror
Pastry cutters
Cork for backing – slightly larger than size of mirror
Strong adhesive
Paintbrush
Varnish brush

EASY LEVEL

DOUGH-COIL MIRROR

The first project in this chapter is the simplest of mirror frames. As long as you cook it at the lowest oven setting and avoid extremes of temperature, it can be baked like any other object.

Although the dough for most of the projects in this book is rolled out to a thickness of ¼in (5mm), it is impossible to be this precise with mirrors. Modern, ⅛in (3.5mm) mirrors can be too thick and heavy for ¼in (5mm) dough. Use your judgement and adjust the thickness of the dough according to the size of mirror. As a general rule, use a ⅜in (1cm) dough base for all mirrors of "average" thickness.

As always, air-drying is a good alternative to baking. Leave your mirror in a warm place – an airing cupboard is ideal – where it will not be disturbed. Check on it every day, and use the tap test (*see pp. 8-15*) to see if it is ready.

When baking, put the mirror into a cold oven and let it heat up with the mirror inside. When it is baked, leave your model inside the oven as it slowly cools down again.

EASY LEVEL

CUT-OUT FRAME

This frame could not be simpler to make, or easier to adapt. Wire loops embedded in the back of the frame hold photographs or pictures in place, and the surround uses two different sizes of pastry cutter, so there is no need for any freehand measuring or cutting at all. Use pairs of matching cutters in different sizes, or even differently-shaped cutters to vary the type of frame – a circle with a smaller heart shape inside, perhaps, or a square with a star. As long as there is a significant difference in size between the cutters (sufficient to make the surround), the cutter shapes can be as complimentary, or as odd, as you like.

The shape of the frame will inspire the decoration you choose. This scalloped, or fluted, square is emphasized with loops and coils in relief. Scoring texture into the dough with a knife can be effective, or try pressing out tiny cutter shapes to attach and paint.

If you are in doubt about looping and bending wire, refer to the chapter dealing with materials and techniques (*see pp. 8-15*).

1

2

3

4

MATERIALS
Non-stick baking sheet
Rolling pin
Small kitchen knife
Small wooden spatula
Small jar of dough paste
Paintbrush for dough paste
Plus
Different-sized pastry cutters
1mm wire and thinner fuse wire
Wire cutters
Round-ended pliers
Paintbrush
Varnish brush

1 Roll the dough to a thickness of ¼in (5mm). Use the larger cutter to press out the shape.

2 Place the smaller of your two cutters in the centre of the square and press the dough out.

3 Take the 1mm wire and cut a length of about 1-2in (3-4cm) and use the pliers to make a hanging loop. Using the thinner fuse wire, make smaller loops and position them in the middle of each side of the surround. This is now the back of your frame. You will eventually bend these loops of fuse wire inward to hold a picture

or photograph securely in place when the frame is finished.

4 Bake the frame until it is hard enough to handle without distorting its shape. Turn the frame over. While the frame is still warm, roll out dough coil decorations and attach them with dough paste – the heat will help to seal the coils. Return the frame to the oven and keep a close eye on the dough until the decorations have properly hardened and sealed. When the frame is thoroughly cool, paint and then varnish it.

1 Roll the dough out to a thickness of about ⅜in (1cm). With a knife, cut a base measuring about 6½ x 8in (16.5 x 20cm).

2 Now position your mirror in the centre of the base and press it down into the dough.

3 Roll out more dough to a thickness of ¼in (5mm). Cut it to exactly the same size as the base and lay it over the top of the base and mirror so that they are evenly covered. Seal all the edges carefully with dough paste. Cut out an oblong a little more than 1in (3cm) smaller all round than the mirror and carefully peel away the surplus dough to expose the mirror below. Seal the edges with dough paste and clean the mirror with cotton buds.

4 Using wire cutters, cut lengths of 1mm wire and bend them into coils with the pliers.

5 Score a line in the dough around the mirror, about ⅛in (3mm) in from the edge.

6 Embed the wire coils in the frame. Place the mirror in a cold oven and then turn the oven on. When baked, turn the oven off and allow the dough and mirror to cool down. This avoids subjecting the glass to sudden temperature changes, which may cause it to crack. When the dough is thoroughly cool, paint and varnish it. Attach cork backing if desired using a strong adhesive.

1

5

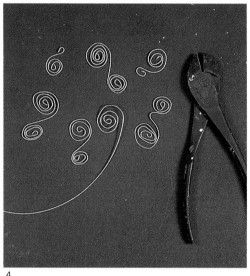

4

3

6

2

MATERIALS
Non-stick baking sheet
Ruler
Rolling pin
Small kitchen knife
Small wooden spatula
Small jar of dough paste
Paintbrush for dough paste
Plus
Mirror – 5 x 7in (13 x 18cm)
Cotton buds
1mm wire
Wire cutters and pliers
Cork for backing
Strong adhesive
Paintbrush
Varnish brush

INTERMEDIATE LEVEL

METAL-COIL MIRROR

Up until now, wire has been used as a material for hanging and threading crafts, but it has decorative qualities, too. This mirror features coils of 1mm wire pressed into the dough to make an unusual finish. The coils themselves are made by curling lengths of wire around the head of a pair of pliers.

To make sure that the decorations are firmly attached to your frame, press them in place and then lever them out carefully and apply a strong adhesive before putting them back.

Bake metal decorations only. If you want to use plastic beads, for example, press them in place, remove them before baking and glue them back when the mirror is cool. Air-drying the dough circumvents this problem.

For a more opulent effect, use beads, sequins and/or coloured glass, but try not to press the dough too hard when embedding these decorative finishes.

Keep a close eye on the baking process. A thick base, a mirror and an extra layer of dough surround will take longer to harden than other projects.

INTERMEDIATE LEVEL

FLORAL FRAME

This attractive frame is designed to be freestanding, rather than hung on a wall. You could either prop it up on a mantleshelf or display shelf, or carefully attach a wire plate stand to the back of the frame and display it at an angle.

The surround has been decorated with shapes produced by small sweet cutters, but you could just as easily make your own shapes by cutting them out freehand. If you are not confident enough for that, try using lids from tubes, spice jars, small bottles, in fact anything with an attractive shape and an appropriate scale. If you would rather work on something smaller, or larger, simply adjust the proportions accordingly, or make a few at a time and produce matching sets of frames.

Once you have created the basic frame, the colour finish is entirely a matter of personal taste and preference. Rich tones and deep, metallic finishes are probably better suited to exotic-looking frames. The simple daisy-shaped cut-outs on this surround lend themselves more to vivid colours, for a bright and cheerful finish.

1

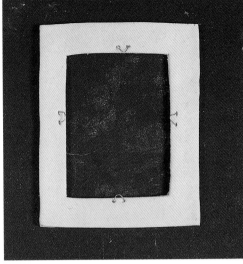

2

3

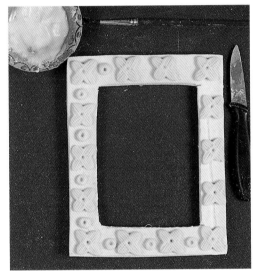

4

MATERIALS

Non-stick baking sheet
Ruler
Rolling pin
Small kitchen knife
Small wooden spatula
Small jar of dough paste
Paintbrush for dough paste
Plus
Small sweet or pastry cutters
Thin, flexible fuse wire
Wire cutters
Round-ended pliers
Paintbrush
Varnish brush

1 Roll out the dough to a thickness of about ⅕in (5mm) – you are now working on your project face down. Cut an oblong, approximately 6½ x 8in (16.5 x 20.5cm). From the centre of this dough, cut a shape measuring about 4 x 5½in (10 x 14cm). With a small spatula, smooth and pat down any uneven edges. Your frame surround should now measure about 2⅖in (6cm) all the way around.

2 Cut four pieces of thin fuse wire – each a little more than 1in (3cm) long – and make four

hooks (*see pp. 8-15*) using the round-ended pliers. Position and embed the hooks in the dough as shown here.

3 Roll out more dough to a thickness of about ⅛in (3mm). Cut out the relief shapes with a sweet cutter, or whatever you are using as a template. Cover these shapes with a towel to prevent them drying out. Bake your frame until it is hard enough to handle without its shape distorting. Turn the frame over and attach the cut-out relief shapes and dough beads with dough paste. If possible, it is

best to do this while the frame is still warm, since the heat helps the pieces to form a tight seal.

4 Add scoring detail using a sharp kitchen knife and make indentations in the centres of the flowers with the handle end of a paintbrush. Return the frame to the oven until the relief decorations are baked and sealed to the base. When the dough is thoroughly cool, paint and varnish it.

1 Choose a plate, about 1¾in (4cm) larger than the mirror you intend to use. Roll the dough out to a thickness of about ⅖in (1cm) and carefully cut around the plate with a sharp knife. Smooth any rough edges.

2 Position your mirror in the centre of the dough and press down, taking care not to distort the circular shape of the surround.

3 Roll out more dough to a thickness of ¼in (5mm). Cut around the plate to make another circle exactly the same as the first. Drape the circle of dough over a rolling pin and lower it over the dough base and mirror. Seal all the outside edges with dough paste. Position the template in the exact centre of dough circle and cut around it with a knife. Smooth and seal the edges around mirror.

4 Taking care not to press right through the dough, score zig-zag details around the edges of the frame, overlapping the moon tail outlines at top and bottom of the mirror and the nostril curls.

5 To make the cheeks, cut circles ⅛in (3mm) thick, using the lid of a spice jar. Attach them with dough paste and score line details around the edges.

6 Roll dough balls for the eyes and indent the centres (insert metal beads if desired). Roll dough pieces and coil them up for the eyelids and brows. Place the mirror into a cold oven, turn on and bake. When it is baked, let the oven cool down with the mirror inside (or air-dry). When it is cool, paint and varnish. Keep a close eye on the baking process. A thicker base, mirror and an extra layer of dough surround will take longer to harden than some other projects.

2

1

4

3

6

5

MATERIALS

Non-stick baking sheet

Rolling pin

Small kitchen knife

Small wooden spatula

Small jar of dough paste

Paintbrush for dough paste

Plus

Cardboard template
(*see pp. 98-109*)

Mirror

Cotton buds

Cork for backing

Strong adhesive

Paintbrush

Varnish brush

ADVANCED LEVEL

MOON MIRROR

The shape of this mirror surround is perfect for a moon theme. Specific measurements are not given, since sizes depend on the size of the mirror used – choose a plate a little larger in size to make the base and surround. This project recycles an old mirror taken from a chipped frame; a dinner plate gives the shape for the base and surround.

The moon employs straightforward techniques, but its success relies on careful joining and a neat finish. If you have the confidence to go for a bold paint effect, the end result is guaranteed to be spectacular.

Although instructions are given for baking, you may find air-drying more convenient (and less expensive) than monopolizing the oven and spending money on fuel.

By now you should be experienced enough to put other craft skills to use. Varying the size of the template to fit a smaller or larger mirror and cutting around an appropriately sized bowl, dish or plate should be no problem, especially if you are keen to reuse a mirror you can't bear to throw away!

MATERIALS
Non-stick baking sheet
Rolling pin
Small kitchen knife
Small wooden spatula
Small jar of dough paste
Paintbrush for dough paste
Pastry brush
Plus
Star-shaped pastry/sweet cutter
1mm wire
Wire cutters
Round-ended pliers
Paintbrush
Varnish brush

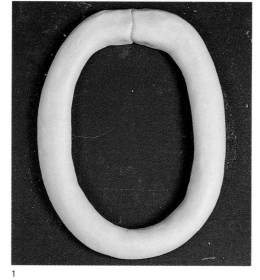

1

2

SHELL FRAME

This final project in the book is loaded with shells and starfish. Too neat a composition, however, and the wreath could look very static. Instead, arrange the shells and starfish in natural groups and the effect will be realistic enough to have been swept ashore by the sea.

Modelling cockleshells and screw-shells by hand is not difficult. The exact technique is explained in detail in the chapter dealing with materials and techniques (*see pp. 8-15*). It is a good idea to practise making these before tackling this project.

As always with projects that involve using thicker dough, air-drying can be more economical than baking. Make sure that you put the frame in a warm, dry atmosphere, somewhere where it won't be jolted or moved. Leave it to dry and then use the tap test (*see pp. 8-15*) to check when it is ready.

Whether you air-dry or bake, browning the frame off in the oven will produce a very natural-looking finish. Keep an eye on your frame until it has "toasted" to the colour and tone you desire, and then lightly brush it with an uneven finish of fine gold paint and then varnish.

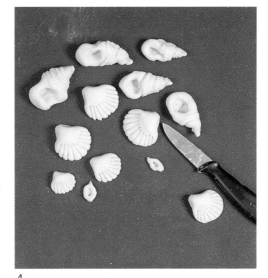

4

5

3

6

1 Roll out a sausage of dough about 16½in (42cm) long and 1in (2.5cm) wide. Working straight on to the baking tray, join the roll to make an oval shape. Squeeze the dough gently to join it, or use some dough paste if necessary.

2 With a rolling pin, flatten the dough out to an even thickness of about ¼in (5mm). Use your own judgement to even out the oval. Use a knife to cut away surplus dough.

3 This is now the back of your frame. Using pliers, loop four pieces of 1⅝in (4cm) long wire and embed the ends into the top, bottom, right and left sides of the frame. Bake or air-dry.

4 Model the shells by hand (*see pp. 8-15*). Give yourself a good selection from which to choose by making more than you need. Cover them with a towel until they are needed.

5 Roll some dough out to a thickness of ⅛in (3mm) and cut out relief shapes using a star pastry cutter. Smooth any rough edges with a spatula. Cover these with a towel until they are needed.

6 When the frame is baked (or air-dried) and hard enough to handle without distorting, turn it over. Use dough paste to attach the shells and stars to the frame in groups in a natural way. Turn up the edges of the stars and score the surfaces. Use tiny shell shapes to fill any spaces. Return the frame to the oven until the shells have sealed and taken on the right shade of brown. When the dough is thoroughly cool, brush it with a little gold paint just to highlight the surface details. Allow it to dry and then varnish.

MAKING TEMPLATES

If you are new to dough craft modelling, you will find the photographs of
the finished projects and the step-by-
step pictures of the pieces being made
useful as a guide for your initial
attempts. However, you will no doubt
very soon wish to branch out and put
some of your own ideas to the test.

When making models you should
handle the dough as little as possible to
prevent it spoiling, so it is vital to have
a clear idea of the sizes and shapes of
all the component pieces and the way
they fit together, before you start to
work. The first step, then, is to produce a full-sized sketch of how you
imagine your finished model will look,
like the ones shown here. The more
detailed these sketches are the better,
because you can use them not only as a
guide for making templates (*see pp.
100-109*) but also as a colour chart for
painting your model when it is baked
and completely cooled.

MAKING TEMPLATES

The templates on the pages that follow mostly relate to the models in the projects chapters of the book. Some others, however, have been included simply as useful shapes, which you may want to incorporate into your own modelling ideas. Templates are extremely straightforward to make. Try not to rush the tracing and cutting processes, however, since well-made templates produce better results and can be used time and time again.

MATERIALS
Cardboard
(old cereal boxes are ideal)
Sharp pencil
Craft knife or scissors
Non-scratch surface for cutting
Tracing paper

● Trace the shapes carefully on to tracing paper.

● Place the tracing paper on the cardboard and, using a sharp pencil, draw over the traced shape, pressing firmly enough to leave an impression of the outline on the cardboard beneath.

● Use a craft knife or scissors to cut around the shapes.

● Alternatively, cut out photocopies of the template shapes, lay them on a piece of cardboard, and cut carefully around them.

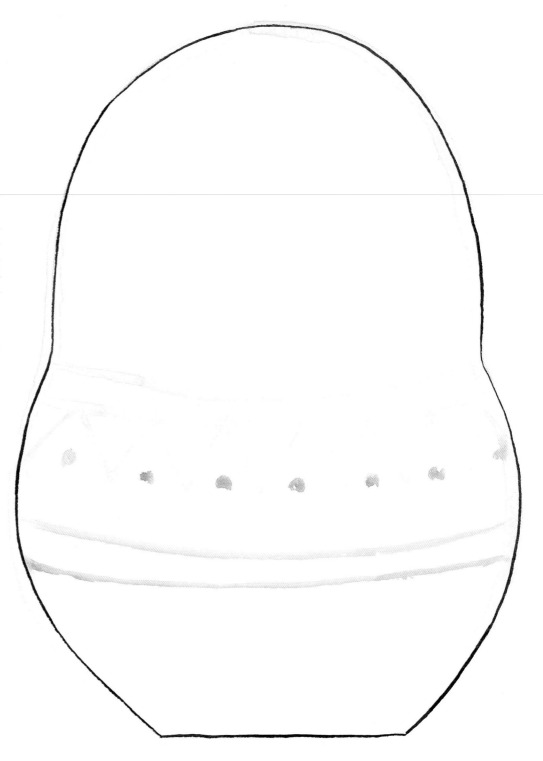

VASE OF SUNFLOWERS

100

CAT

SHEEP

FLOWER

DUCK

FISH

LEAF

WHITE RABBIT

Face

Waistcoat

Belly

Cheek relief

Legs

SUN BOOKENDS

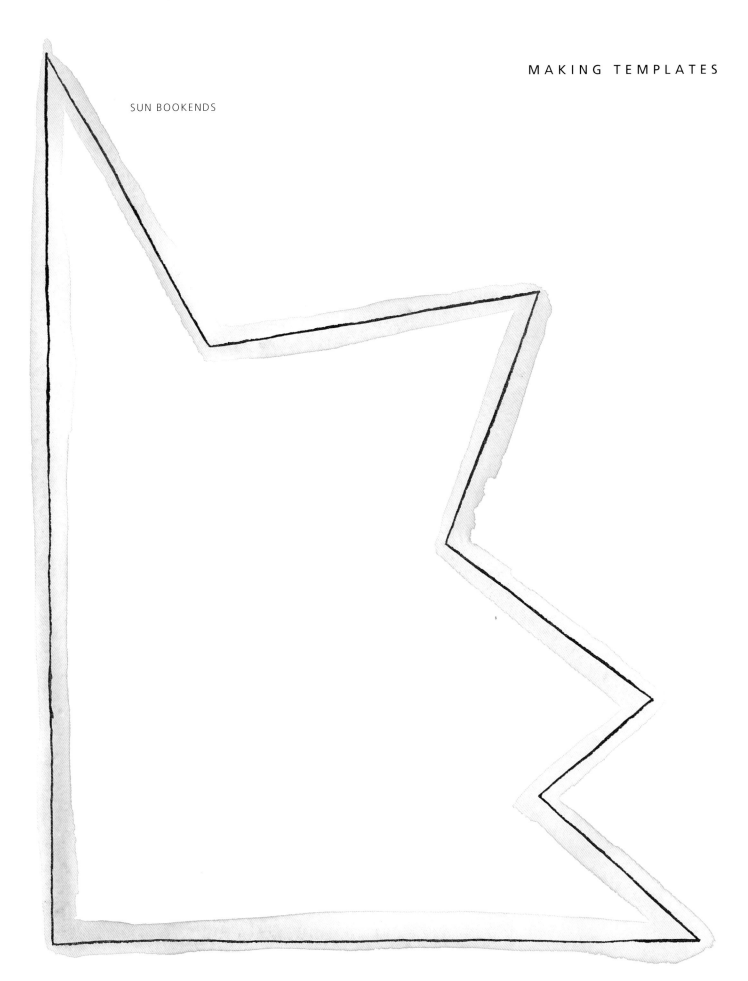

MOTHER GOOSE

Wing

Beak

Scarf

Feet

Apron

Wing

COW JUMPED OVER THE MOON

Face

Thigh

Moon

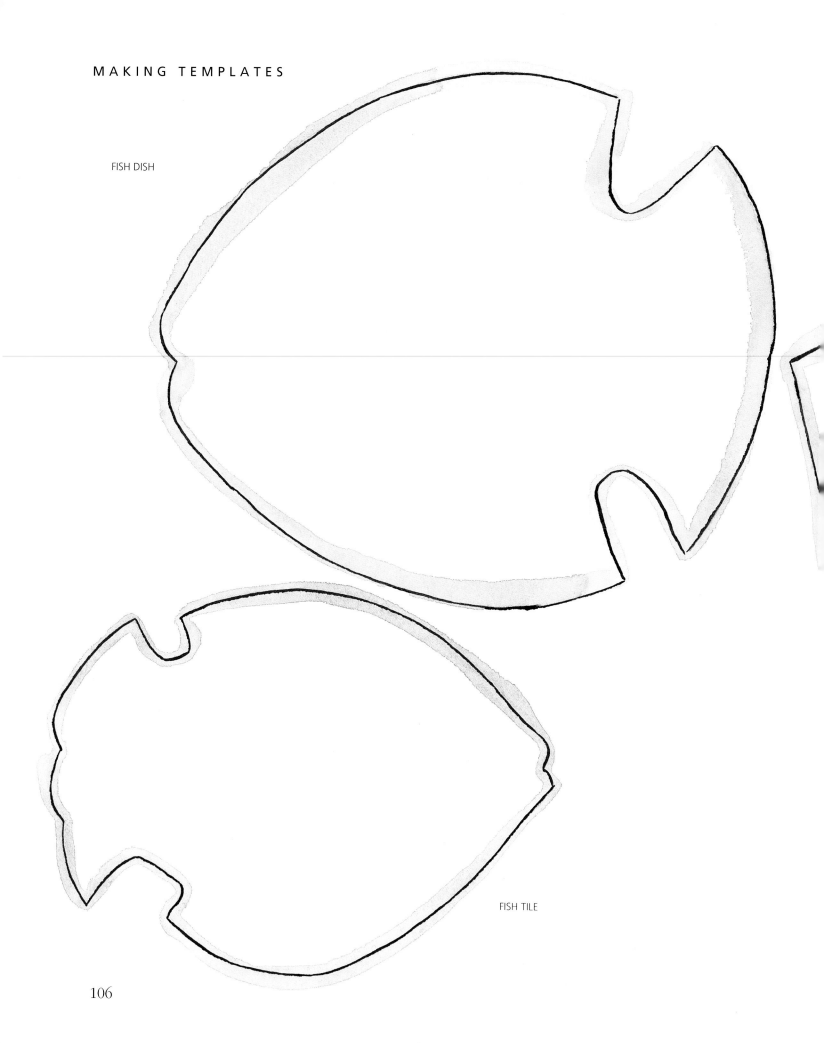

FISH DISH

FISH TILE

FISH WREATH

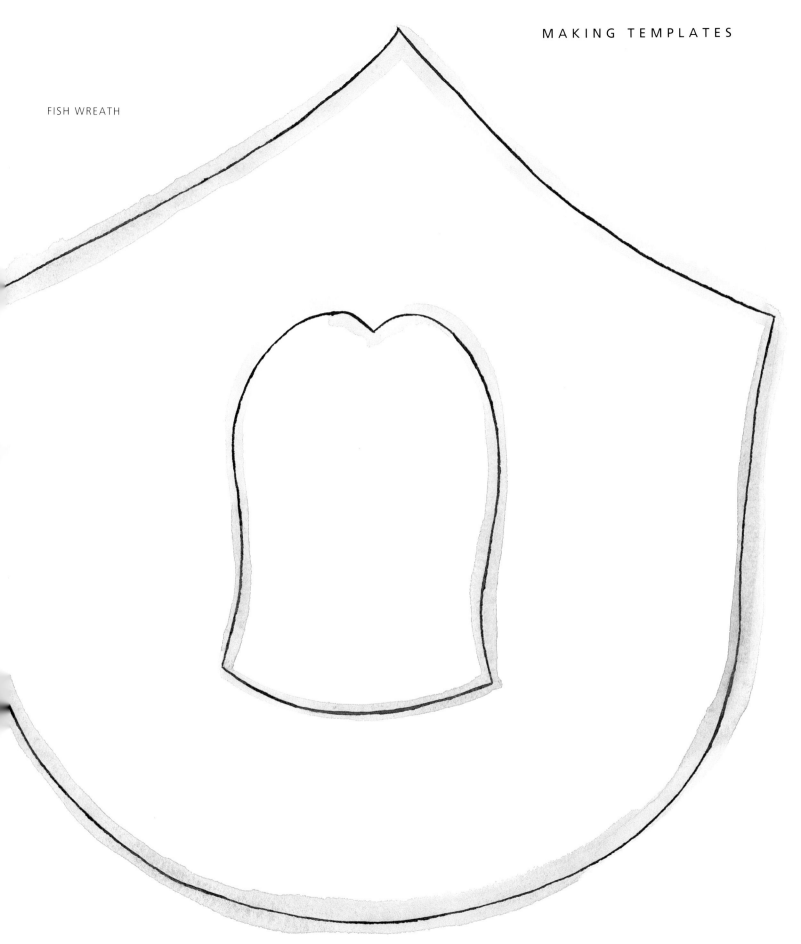

HEARTS

HEART PLAQUE

HANGING HEARTS/
VALENTINE DISH

HANGING HEARTS/
VALENTINE DISH

HANGING HEARTS

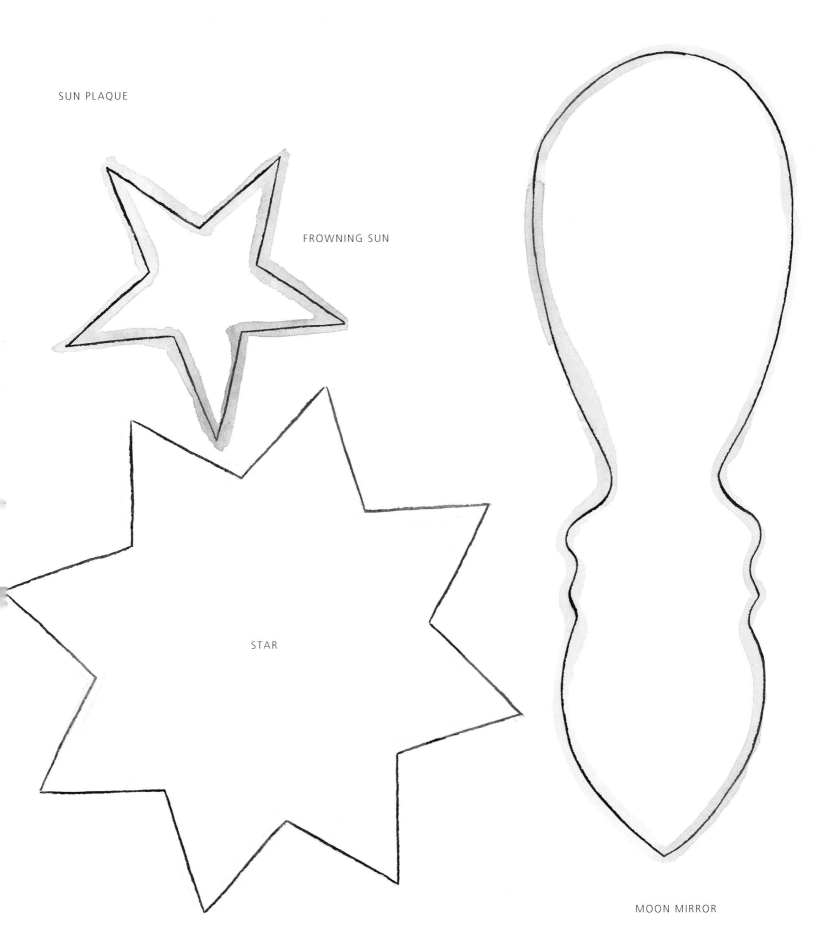

SUN PLAQUE

FROWNING SUN

STAR

MOON MIRROR

109

INDEX

ACKNOWLEDGEMENTS

THE PUBLISHERS AND AUTHOR WOULD LIKE TO THANK THE
FOLLOWING PEOPLE AND ORGANIZATIONS FOR THEIR GENEROUS HELP
AND SUPPORT IN THE PRODUCTION OF THIS BOOK:

SUPPLIER OF ACCESSORIES AND PROPS

THE DINING ROOM SHOP
62-64 WHITE HART LANE
BARNES
LONDON SW13 OP2

SPECIAL THANKS TO

KATHIE GILL FOR INDEXING

SANDRA AND PETER, NICK AND CAROLINE, AND JENNY AND STEWART
FOR THE USE OF THEIR HOMES FOR PHOTOGRAPHY